A FIELD GUIDE TO THE

Wildflowers
and Common Trees
of East Africa

By: Dr. David J. Allen

Designed and produced by:
Camerapix Publishers International
PO Box 45048, 00100 GPO
Nairobi, Kenya

© David J. Allen, 2007

ISBN: 1-904722-28-8

Printed in Singapore.

Cover: (left) Fig. 71 Sand Olive (*Dodonaea angustifolia*),
(right) Fig. 113 Blue Bog Lobelia (*Lobelia deckenii*)
(Photo: Tore Hagen), (middle) Fig. 24 Glory Lily (*Gloriosa superba*)
(Photo: Andrew Beckett), (bottom) Acacia silhouetted against red sky
(Photo: Karl Ammann).

Back Cover: The Author, on Mount Meru (Photo: Simon Carter).

CONTENTS	PAGE

LIST OF ILLUSTRATIONS

8

Front Cover (bottom): Acacia silhouetted against red sky (Photo: Karl Ammann).

Back Cover: The Author, on Mount Meru
          (Photo: Simon Carter)

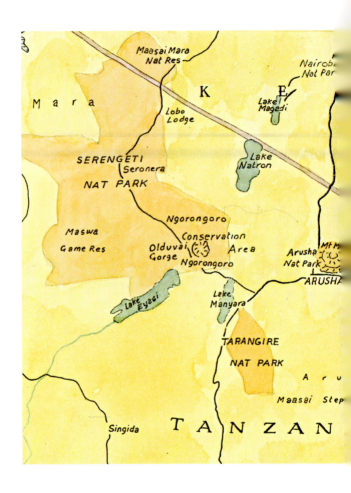

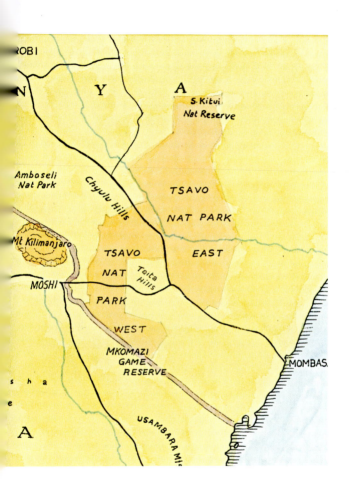

FOREWORD

A 'Safari' is a Swahili word meaning 'a journey', and a journey through East Africa is a true assault on the senses: a kaleidoscope of sights, sounds and smells. Going on safari, the first thought is normally to see those landmarks of the continent: the big cats, the elephants, the huge grazing herds, but visitors quickly realise there are other, equally important facets; for without the grasslands and flowers, trees and bushes, the wide scope and unimaginably beautiful vistas of Africa, it would be nothing, and indeed, the habitats to support those awe-inspiring animals, simply would not exist.

I can think of no better person than Dr. David Allen to write a guide on the wealth of wildflowers and trees one sees on a safari in East Africa. Having spent many an hour exploring kopjes, walking across the plains and investigating the forests of Tanzania in the company of David, I am constantly amazed by his knowledge and infectious enthusiasm for his subject.

This booklet will allow the visitor to the region to have an informative, easy-to-read guide, bursting with information, and yet easily carried out into the field on safari. This information includes not only identification guides but also medicinal and local uses of a plant, all described in David's easily understood but authoritative manner.

For anyone with an interest in Africa, for anyone on safari, and even for safari guides like myself, who encourage those on safari to look well beyond the 'Big Five', this booklet will be an invaluable addition to their library and to their understanding of the region.

Andrew Beckett,
Journey Into Africa

PREFACE

This booklet has had a long gestation. Sometime in 1989, the idea for it emerged from animated discussion one evening with Alfred Leo of Lions Safaris. Material for it has been gathered slowly, reinforced by sporadic sorties into the bush, with Barry Smithson, Simon Carter and David Gundry, then with Glyn and Debby Lewis of Sengo Safaris, with Andrew and Shelly Beckett, once with Rangers Safaris and now of Journey into Africa, and most recently also with Gary and Jo Strand of Wildlife Explorer who deserve special thanks for outstanding hospitality. For literature, I have relied most heavily upon Agnew's *Flora of Upland Kenya*, Blundell's *Wild Flowers of East Africa* and on Beentje's *Trees, Shrubs and Lianas of Kenya*. These and other important sources of information are listed in Literature Cited and Further reading which amounts to a fairly extensive bibliography that may prove useful to the academic reader. But I hasten to add that I alone remain responsible for such errors, inaccuracies and other imperfections that remain.

My purpose has been to produce a truly pocket-size booklet that describes and illustrates many of the more important, common or conspicuous species of wild flower and tree likely to be met with on safari. My focus is the northern parks and wildlife reserves of Tanzania that I know best, from Mkomazi in the East westwards to Ngorongoro, Loliondo and the Serengeti. Mount Kilimanjaro, Arusha National Park and Mount Meru, Lake Manyara and Tarangeri are also covered. But the booklet also has obvious relevance to the wildlife areas of Kenya that border northern Tanzania, including Tsavo West, the Taita Hills, the Chyulu Hills, Amboseli and the Maasai Mara (map, page 10-11). For this reason, we have chosen to use 'East Africa' in the title of the book. With a few exceptions, these are the places that most visitors go to when on safari. But we make no pretence that the whole of East Africa is covered. Coverage of plant species also cannot hope to be anything other than partial: it is estimated that there may be over 10,000 species of flowering plant in Tanzania alone. What follows is a largely subjective selection of only about 100 of the species representative of ecological zones from that vast diversity. An ecological arrangement seemed a better basis for the book's structure than one in which species are grouped taxonomically by family, or by flower colour. But readers should bear in mind that some species can be found in a variety of habitats, so that the placement of a species under the heading of one ecological zone rather than another may at times seem somewhat arbitrary.

Treatment of individual species follows a format that begins with a description of the plant followed by an indication of its geographical and ecological distribution. I have chosen also to include some mention of the cultural place of each species under the heading of 'Interest'; for the uses of wild plants are often part of ancient traditions and are part of cultural heritage, whether as a source of fibre, food or herbal medicine, a dye, an oil or as a decorative. I have given some vernacular names, in Swahili and Maasai in addition to English, wherever possible. Decisions on what common names to use have sometimes been difficult, and I have often had no alternative than to anglicize the scientific name when no vernacular name exists. In general, I have tried to avoid using technical terms except where it seemed absolutely necessary; a Glossary is given to explain those words that have slipped into the text.

Whereas the Tanzania National Parks ('TANAPA') guides, and now Veronica Roodt's booklets deal with a wide range of wildlife, including flowers and trees, pocket books on the vegetation alone are scanty. The *Flora of Tropical East Africa* is the ultimate source and also Blundell's excellent guide is fairly comprehensive and well-illustrated, the former is aimed at the specialist and the latter is also comparatively bulky and its content could seem bewildering in its coverage to the average tourist.

Sapiehe's *Wayside Flowers of Kenya* lies at the other end of the scale: it is certainly pocket-size and nicely illustrates those few species covered, but it is very limited both in its scope and scientific substance. In between these extremes lies Jex-Blake's *Some Wild Flowers of Kenya* published in 1948. Its substance is more sound but dated and now difficult to obtain. There is a dearth of other books that would serve as a traveller's guide to the area. This booklet is designed to fill that niche.

The majority of the illustrations are my own; those that are not are all acknowledged in the List of Illustrations. An exception is the map, presented on p. 10-11, which has been drafted by Alan Jackson. I also thank Andrew Beckett for writing the Foreword, and my wife Leonora who has not only shared in so many of our safaris but has typed most expertly from my manuscript.

Dr. David J. Allen
July, 2006

INTRODUCTION

Some Geology

Africa is unimaginably old. Some of the oldest rocks on earth are found in the Serengeti, thought to be 2-3 billion years old. The East African plateaulands, which are mostly over 1,300 m (4,260 feet) above sea level, are composed fundamentally of what is known as Archaean Basement rock. Some parts have been affected by intrusions of granite, revealed as tumbled masses of boulders (inselbergs or 'kopjes') that are a striking feature of the landscape (Fig. 1).

Elsewhere on the plateau, the basement is covered with sedimentary rocks, including schists and quartzites of pre-Cambrian age. Intensive folding occurred here in pre-Cambrian times, more than 570 million years ago. Although there is evidence of faults also in post-Jurassic and Tertiary times, the Rift Valley landscape of East Africa is comparatively recent, occurring in the Pleistocene, well after the appearance of Man in East Africa. About 5 million years ago, the rift opened and lava gushed out and spread to form the Ngorongoro Crater Highlands. During the volcanic activity that followed, Ngorongoro reached an altitude of 5,000 m (16,400 feet), blasting ash and rock debris over a huge area. Now, Ngorongoro is a vast volcanic crater (Fig. 2), about 20 km (12 miles) across with a floor of over 100 square miles. This makes it the world's sixth largest caldera, but it is the largest unflooded, unbroken one. The crater now lies nestled in a range of extinct volcanoes up to about 3,050 m (10,000 feet).

Layer upon layer of volcanic ash settled over the Serengeti Plains to the West of the highlands, forming a flat skin of ash penetrated only by the granite kopjes as reminders of the ancient basement buried beneath. Over time, rainfall has leached the salts from the surface layers so as to form a hardpan that is impenetrable to plant roots, so preventing the growth of trees but enabling colonization by a sward of shallow rooted grasses.

Fig. 1 Kopjes are intrusions of granite that are striking features of the plains.

A ribbon of lakes now fills the line of the rift, from Lake Magadi which lies at an altitude of 580 m (1,900 feet) southwest of Nairobi, southwards across the Kenya-Tanzania border to Lake Natron and Lake Manyara. Lake Eyasi rests in a south-western branch. All have a high alkaline content, reflected in the name 'magadi' which means soda in Swahili. Whereas there is no pronounced escarpment to the east of Lake Magadi, there is an imposing wall to the rift that towers above Lake Manyara on its western shore (Fig. 3).

Amid the terrestrial confusion during the formation of the Great Rift Valley, East Africa's other great volcanoes were formed, including Mount Meru (4,600 m; 14,978 feet), Kilimanjaro (5,895 m; 19,340 feet) and Mount Kenya (5,199 m; 17,058 feet), all between about two and a half and three million years ago. Ol-Doinyo Lengai, meaning 'Mountain of God' in Maasai, lies just south of Lake Natron, and is one of the few active volcanoes. Meru and the main peak (Kibo) of Kilimanjaro are dormant; Kilimanjaro's second peak (Mawenzi) and Mount Kenya are extinct. Mount Meru, which towers imposingly above Arusha was once much higher. Its name in Maasai means 'that which does not make a noise'. There is evidence that Meru's crater once contained a deep lake. When the ash-cone was thrust up (Fig. 4), molten magma from the bowels of the earth mixed with lake water, turning to steam. Huge pressure led to a colossal explosion in which the entire eastern wall of the crater was blown apart.

The Usambara Mountains near Tanga, are of non-volcanic origin and are part of the ancient crystalline complex consisting of gneiss that underlies reddish brown soils typically low in potash and calcium.

The rocks of East Africa provided early Man with a variety of materials for making tools, from obsidian to small deposits of iron. And it is in the Rift Valley that most of the important fossils have been found. Olduvai Gorge is the best known site in our area (Fig. 5).

Climate and Season

In East Africa, the dead season is governed by the lack of soil moisture, not by low temperatures as in the North. North-eastern monsoon winds, called the Kaskazi, prevail from November to March then, from April, wind direction changes to the south-east. The rain these easterly winds bring from the Indian Ocean makes coastal areas some of the most favourable environments anywhere, reflected in their extraordinary degree of plant diversity and endemism. Inland, in the semi-arid and montane areas with which we are concerned here, rain falls in a bimodal pattern as a result of oscillations of the Inter-tropical Convergence Zone, where the two air masses of the south-east and north-east trades meet. The Long Rains, or masika, season is usually from April to June and the Short Rains, or vuli, from October to December. Over our area, there are essentially two dry seasons, from January to March and from July to September. Superimposed upon this pattern is the close connection of rainfall and relief, or altitude, the higher areas being much better watered. But soil moisture is governed ultimately by the potential evaporation rate which in general exceeds rainfall; and it is soil moisture more than any other environmental factor that controls the development of vegetation.

Plant Ecology and Adaptation

The great range of ecology and climate in our area underlies the vast diversity in the flora of the region. Not only is East Africa rich in the number of species but also in the range of adaptive strategies employed to survive in those diverse habitats. For instance, survival in the seasonally arid bushland may rely on some mechanism of water storage, in a bulbous stem base as in Desert Rose (p. 36) or a water-retentive trunk as in Baobab (p. 54). Protection against browsing may be afforded by spines, by employing armies of ants as sentries, or 'askaris' (p. 76), or in the rapid synthesis of an unpalatable or toxic chemical, examples of all of which occur in species of Acacia. African acacias can even warn one another of predation, by releasing ethylene gas which is detected by other acacias, stimulating them also to produce poison so that foliage is no longer palatable to browsing animals.

Fig. 2 Ngorongoro Crater is the world's largest unflooded, unbroken caldera.

Fire is a regular feature of semi-arid environments, so that fire resistance has evolved in vegetation adapted here. Whistling Thorn (p. 76) has thick, corky bark, long bare trunks and canopies held high to reduce vulnerability to fire, whereas Xerophyta (p. 66) has a fibrous stem that protects against bush fires. At the onset of the rains, the fibre immediately re-absorbs moisture and the plant produces flowers within three or four days. Such "resurrection plants" exhibit one of the most remarkable adaptations to dry conditions.

In semi-arid areas, the columnar nests of termites ("white ants") can be conspicuous (Fig. 6). Termites forage widely and are often damaging, for instance, to fence posts and buildings. But termites play a significant role in the functioning of savannahs, as consumers and agents of nutrient transfer. Their life-styles include some remarkable associations that are beneficial to both partners. Termites can live symbiotically with certain bacteria that are able to fix atmospheric nitrogen and may play a role in enhancing soil fertility locally. Furthermore, termites also have a symbiotic association with fungi. The masticated woody material from which termites' nests are made supplies nourishment to the edible mushroom genus *Termitomyces* species of which have specific, obligate associations with termites. The termites cultivate the fungal mycelium in fungus gardens, and termite nymphs sometimes graze on these gardens like miniature sheep!

In riverine forest, the Sausage Tree (p. 144) possesses large, dark red and malodorous flowers which attract fruit bats that pollinate them. Location of the flowers by bats is thought to be assisted also by ultrasound echoes from the flowers that hang isolated beneath the canopy on long stalks. Here too, there is another even more highly evolved adaptation which is among the most intimate of relationships between a plant and its pollinator, found between the Sycamore Fig and a species of gall wasp (p. 126). In sub-montane forest, another species of fig (p. 172) makes its living as a strangler. Initially, they grow slowly, entwining a branch of a forest tree while feeding off the debris

Fig. 3 The Great Rift Valley: the wall to the rift above the western shore of Lake Manyara.

accumulated around their roots. Their roots then extend along their host's branch to surround its trunk, fusing to form a lattice. When the roots reach the ground, the fig is able to harness nutrients in the soil and grows more rapidly. Now it embraces the trunk with more and more of its aerial roots, appearing to strangle the host tree. In due course, the host tree dies, in part through starvation from competition for light, but the fig's lattice of roots has by this time formed a strong cylinder and it is now an independent component of the forest.

At higher altitude again, now in the Afro-alpine Zone, where the soil surface is extremely mobile because of nightly ice formation and frost-heaving alternating with thawing each day, seedling establishment must be extremely hazardous. Haplocarpha (p. 226) has overcome this obstacle by burying its fruit while still attached to the plant. Another problem facing plants in the Afro-alpine zone is how to survive freezing temperatures at night and yet be able to withstand baking equatorial sun during the day, on a more or less constant *diurnal* rhythm wherein it is "winter every night and summer every day". The solution appears to be gigantism, as strikingly demonstrated by the groundsels (p. 232). Giant groundsels have dense rosettes of leaves at the tip of branched stems. As the branches grow, the ring of leaves dies but remains attached so as to form lagging around the trunk to protect the water-conducing tissues from freezing whereas the living leaves produce a sort of 'anti-freeze'. But the retention of dead leaves deprives the roots of nutrients that would otherwise have been released into the soil from decomposition of the leaf tissue. This further problem is overcome by the development from the side of the trunk of adventitious roots, which then extract what nutrients can be found within the lagging. Remarkably, a similar gigantism has evolved in the high equatorial Andes.

Biodiversity and Endemism

The African flora is immensely rich. It has been estimated that the continent as a whole may have about 63,000 species of flowering plant and fern.

Fig. 4 Mount Meru: the ash cone is a reminder of the one-time terrestrial confusion (Photo: Simon Carter).

Inter-tropical Africa has some 30,000 species of which 40% are endemic, or unique. Tanzania alone probably has in excess of 10,000 species, 11% of which are endemic. Within our area, Mkomazi has an exceptionally rich flora estimated well in excess of 1,150 species in 120 families; this compares with 955 species recorded from Tsavo East. To the south-east, lie the Usambara Mountains which are thought to have more endemic animal and plant species than any other comparable mountain range in Africa, as a result of their great age, their isolation, and the occasional arrival of colonist species from other parts of Africa. Conversely, the Usambaras have been an important source of colonists for the younger volcanic peaks, like Kilimanjaro.

Montane endemics were once widespread species that have been left behind in those parts of their range where they can compete. The giant lobelias are a case in point. Whereas *Lobelia gibberoa* is a widespread species of forest margins at lower altitudes on many mountains, the Blue Bog Lobelia (*L. deckenii*; see p. 238) has speciated and there are six different sub-species on six different mountain massifs, a radiation that must have occurred rapidly (in less than a million years) on these geologically young volcanoes. Other species, like *Arabis alpina* (p. 242), appear to evolve much more slowly, for this species shows almost no variation over its vast geographical range.

Alien Introductions

There is, of course, a large array of flowering plant species that are deliberate introductions from other continents. Avenue trees including the spectacular mauve flowered Jacaranda, the yellow Cassia (*C. spectabilis*), and common garden decoratives like *Bougainvillea*, Frangipani (*Plumeria rubra*) and Poinsettia (*Euphorbia pulcherrima*) and the coffee shade tree *Grevillea* are all exotics. Commercial crop plants like Sisal (*Agave sisalana*), protective hedging like Prickly Pear (*Opuntia vulgaris*) and pernicious weeds including Mexican Poppy (*Argemone mexicana*), Apple of Peru (*Nicandra physalodes*) and Mexican

Fig. 5 Olduvai Gorge: the best known site where fossil finds of early man have been made.

Marigold (*Tagetes minuta*) are all introduced species. With the exception of *Grevillea* which comes from Australia, all are tropical American in origin.

Vegetation Zones

There are no deserts in East Africa nor are there semi-deserts within the area covered by this booklet (map, page 10-11). Here, 'semi-arid bushland' refers to the drier areas typified by Mkomazi and Tsavo where shrub or small tree canopy cover is at least 40%. This is the *Acacia-Commiphora* savannah at the southern tip of the Sahel. 'Wooded grassland' is savannah grassland with scattered or grouped trees (Fig. 7) with a canopy cover of 10-40%, typified by much of the Serengeti and the Maasai Mara. Riverine and ground-water forest, along perennial water courses and where the water table is higher, is exemplified in Tarangire and in Lake Manyara National Parks, respectively. Sub-montane and montane forest, within which there is a more-or-less continuous stand of trees with interlocking canopies, are widespread in the Ngorongoro Highlands and on Mounts Kilimanjaro and Meru (Fig. 8). On many of East Africa's mountains, the upper reaches of forest give way to a belt of bamboo, then one of *Hagenia* and Giant St. John's-wort, before the start of the moorland, dominated by Tree Heather (Fig. 9). With increasing altitude again, there is a transition from moorland to the alpine zone, marked by the appearance of Giant Groundsels and Giant Lobelia, and it is the Afro-alpine zone that has an uncanny resemblance to the 'paramo' of the Andes.

Grassland and Grazing

The Serengeti is home to one of the greatest wildlife spectacles on earth, reflected in the area's international designation by UNESCO as a World Heritage Site, as is also Ngorongoro Crater. The two areas provide a striking contrast in terms of grassland and grazing behaviour, as we shall see.

Among the great grasslands of the world, those in East Africa are now the only ones that still support their populations of large grazing animals almost

Fig. 6 The columnar nests of termites can be conspicuous in semi-arid areas.

Fig. 7 Wooded grassland in Tarangire National Park in the dry season.

intact. It is these vast concentrations of wild animals that tourists principally come to see.

In the Ngorongoro Crater, the key to the dense carrying capacity of its grassland is the combination of the extensive marshes created by perennial springs, the comparatively abundant rainfall and the fertility and diversity of soil types underlying the area. Space is sufficient only for a limited population of *resident* animals, well within the limits of productivity of the ecosystem. However, in the Serengeti, rain does not fall uniformly across the area: the south-easterly section, near Naabi Hill, dries out more quickly than the northwest. By May, its grass has been grazed so low that the plains game have to move. Zebra, gazelles and, most famously, a million or so wildebeest begin to migrate towards the northwest, reaching the lush grasslands of the Maasai Mara, in southern Kenya. By November, these plains are beginning to fail but, down in the Serengeti, rain is now beginning again, so the huge herds of wildebeest must trek back once more. So, while the animal populations in the Crater are resident in their 'oasis', those of the Serengeti Plains follow a pattern of migration in response to the rainfall pattern and grass growth. But the plains game don't damage the grassland, in part because they don't stay long enough and partly because grasses themselves can withstand considerable punishment because of the way they grow. The leaf of a grass has its growing point at its base. The plant spreads both by seed and also by horizontal stems along the surface, with leaves sprouting from each joint. The species of grasses in the short grass plains are shallow-rooted perennials that survive the drought of the dry season and yet burst into growth within hours of rainfall, feeding the herds during the wet season. If left ungrazed, the species composition of the grasslands would change, with taller grasses competing out the short ones which have a higher leaf to stem ratio than taller species.

The fact that such a variety of animals can co-exist relates partly to adaptations among individual species to grazing. Even when feeding off the same sort of

Fig. 8 Montane forest on Kilimanjaro.

grass, animals tend to select different portions with varying ratios of leaf to stem, and these differences in diet reflect differences in mouth shape. Thus, the razor-sharp teeth of zebra enable them to bite through the stems of the taller grasses whereas the wide muzzles of wildebeest are well-suited to mowing the short grasses. Gazelles have pointed muzzles adapted to select the youngest shoots. Other animals occupy other niches, so in this way, every part of the environment is exploited.

This evident efficiency in exploiting all niches is yet more sophisticated: there is a grazing succession among migratory populations, led by zebra that select grass stems. Zebra feeding tends to increase the frequency of leaf thereby increasing the suitability of the vegetation for wildebeest that now follow the zebra herds. In turn wildebeest affect the composition of vegetation, favouring its use by gazelles that select small plants other than grasses.

On the grass plain, "the bone of Africa emerges in magnificent outcrops or kopjes ... topped sometimes by huge perched blocks shaped by the wearing away of ages", as beautifully expressed by Peter Matthiessen. In the clefts of kopjes, trapped water collects with both wind-blown soil and eroded rock where tree seeds are able to take root, so that these kopjes become islands of contrasting vegetation, and so too of animals, in the surrounding sea of grass.

It is perhaps worth adding here that wildlife conservation in Tanzania owes much to the fact that 28% of its surface area has some protection, in the form of National Parks (including the Serengeti, Lake Manyara, Tarangire, Mount Meru and Ngurdoto Crater, and Mount Kilimanjaro); Game Reserves (Mkomazi); Conservation Areas (Ngorongoro Crater and Loliondo); Forest Reserves (like Mazumbai Forest in the Western Usambara Mountains); Biosphere Reserves (Serengeti, Ngorongoro and Lake Manyara) and World Heritage Sites (Serengeti and Ngorongoro).

Fig. 9 Moorland on the Shira Plateau, Kilimanjaro.

1. Plants of Dry and Semi-arid Bushland

DESERT ROSE (*Adenium obesum*)
Mwandiga, Mdiga, Mdagu (Swa.)

Periwinkle and Oleander Family (*Apocynaceae*)

Identification: A thickset, succulent shrub or small tree up to about 3 m tall; the lower part of the stem usually bulbous. The bark is smooth, spineless and grey-green. Leaves are obovate to elliptic in outline and are arranged alternately, crowded at the ends of branches; they are somewhat fleshy, hairless, shiny, dark green above and paler beneath, with a prominent midrib. All parts of the plant contain copious watery sap. Flowers, which appear before the leaves, are very showy: they are tubular in form, with white, pink or red petals turned out at the end of the corolla tube. Fruit are paired and cigar-shaped, splitting to release seeds that are oblong with a parachute at both ends, so that the seed is blown along the ground like an axle with two wheels.

Distribution: Widespread throughout tropical Africa where it occurs in dry bushland among rock, in coastal thicket, desert scrub and *Acacia-Commiphora-Combretum* wooded grassland.

Interest: Desert Rose, which resembles a miniature Baobab, is a poisonous plant, like its relatives Oleander, *Acokanthera* and *Strophanthus*, containing cardiac glycosides that interfere with the nervous action of the heart. The bark and fleshy parts of the trunk are used in preparing arrow poison, often mixed with *Strophanthus*, and a bark infusion is used to rid cattle and camels of ticks and lice. It is also used as a fish poison.

Fig. 10 Desert Rose (*Adenium obesum*)

DEAD SEA FRUIT (*Calotropis procera*)
Mpamba Mwitu (Swa.)

Milkweed Family (*Asclepiadaceae*)

Identification: A stout, somewhat succulent shrub or small tree to 4 m tall, with soft woody stems and woolly young shoots with abundant white latex. The large, oblong and rounded leaves clasp the stem, at the apex of which are dense masses of purple, white and violet flowers. Fruit are inflated bladders 10-25 cm across, packed with a mass of hairs attached to the seed.

Distribution: Widespread and common in dry, stony places, in open bush, at roadsides and in other disturbed places liable to seasonal flooding. Used to mark graves, and planted at the coast to stabilize sand.

Interest: The plant is commonly browsed by livestock; it is often considered poisonous but evidence is contradictory. Honey from the nectar is also said to be poisonous, and the latex contains trypsin. Latex mixed with salt is used to clean and remove hairs from leather and has a range of uses in traditional medicine. A root infusion is used against camel cough, and the plant has been used as an insecticide. The seed hairs provide an inferior substitute for kapok, the inner bark yields 'mudar' fibre which makes strong rope (but is difficult to extract), and the wood is used for canoe paddles and fire sticks.

Fig. 11 Dead Sea Fruit (*Calotropis procera*)

CARALLUMA (*Caralluma speciosa*)

Milkweed Family (*Asclepiadaceae*)

Identification: A perennial, decorative succulent, with erect, 4-angled, greyish green stems arising in clusters. Flowers are large, purplish black to dark violet, borne in dense, few-flowered heads.

Distribution: Uncommon: found in dry alkaline country, near Lake Natron and Olduvai Gorge.

Interest: Cultivated as an ornamental succulent.

Fig. 12 Caralluma (*Caralluma speciosa*)

COMMIPHORA (*Commiphora africana*)
Mbambara (Swa.)

Myrrh Family (*Burseraceae*)

Identification: A deciduous, spiny shrub or small tree which remains leafless for much of the year. The outer bark is typically translucent and papery, peeling to expose the underbark which is green (and so can photosynthesize when the tree is leafless). Leaves are 3-foliolate, the terminal leaflet being much the largest, with both upper and lower surfaces velvety. Flowers, in tight clusters, are small and green, turning red; fruit are oblong and pinkish red, containing a single stone covered by a lobed layer of thin red flesh (the pseudoaril) which is much loved by hornbills.

Distribution: There are some *64 species of Commiphora* in East Africa; *C. africana* is among the commonest and is widespread throughout eastern and southern Africa. *Commiphora* is a gregarious genus, and where one species is found, several others are likely to occur. *C. africana* is typical of bushed grassland, dry *Acacia-Commiphora* bushland and coastal thickets.

Interest: Various medicinal properties are attributed to the bark, fruit and, particularly, the resin. Cuttings root easily, and the tree is widely used in hedging and stockades. The leaves contain bitter tannins, presumably accounting for their resistance to browsing by game. The larva of the beetle *Diamphidia*, from which bushmen make their arrow poison, feeds exclusively on this species in southern Africa where it is called Poison-grub commiphora.

Myrrh is a gum resin from *Commiphora myrrha* and a gum from *C. schimperi* is the tick repellant, opoponax.

Fig. 13 Commiphora *(Commiphora africana)*

DESERT DATE, or SIMPLE-THORNED TORCHWOOD
(*Balanites aegyptiaca*)
Mjunju (Swa.), Ol-ngoswa (Maa.)

Desert Date Family (*Balanitaceae*)

Identification: A small, untidy, evergreen tree with simple, unbranched spines and stalked, leathery leaflets in pairs. Yellowish green flowers are borne in small, fragrant clusters in leaf axils and fruit are fleshy, cylindrical and date-like, and yellowish red when ripe.

Distribution: Widespread in dry bushland, bushed grassland and riverine habitats throughout eastern and southern Africa. Abundant near Kajiado.

Interest: The fruit is edible, but very bitter when green and bitter-sweet when ripe, and yields an edible oil. Fruit also provide treatment for liver and spleen complaints, and are used to poison fish, fresh water snails (including bilharzia hosts), larval stages of *Schistosoma*, and waterfleas that carry guinea-worm. One fruit is said to be sufficient to kill all snails in 30 litres of water, valuable because it is non-toxic to man.

Ethiopian baboons at risk of schistosomiasis are known to eat *Balanites* fruit, which are rich in the potent antischistosome diosgenin, while baboons not exposed to the risk do not

An infusion of roots is used as an emetic against malaria, the gum is used to stick arrow and spear-heads on to shafts, the wood is insect resistant and durable so used for tool handles.

Fig. 14 Desert Date *(Balanites aegyptiaca)*

TERMINALIA (*Terminalia brownii*)

Combretum Family (*Combretaceae*)

Identification: Shrub or leafy, deciduous tree, usually 4-5 m (though occasionally much taller), with an attractive layered appearance. Leaves, which are spirally arranged, turn bright red before falling. Flowers are white to cream and unpleasantly scented, and the fruit are smooth, winged and reddish purple; their length is always less than three times the width.

Distribution: *Terminalia brownii* is widely distributed in dry wooded savannah, deciduous bushland on rocky outcrops, and in riverside habitats.

The related Indian Almond, or Mkungu (*Terminalia catappa*), which has large, red fruit that float in seawater, has become widely naturalized at the coast.

Interest: A decoction from the bark is used as an emetic, as a remedy for fevers and colds. The bitter fruits are edible. The wood is hard and durable, used in building, and it produces a good charcoal. The tree is also much used in agroforestry.

Fig. 15 Terminalia (*Terminalia brownii*)

VELVET-LEAVED COMBRETUM (*Combretum molle*)
Ol-mororoi (Maa.)

Combretum Family (*Combretaceae*)

Identification: A deciduous, spreading tree to 10 m tall, with a crooked trunk that branches low down. Leaves are opposite, simple and broadly oval; their distinctive feature is their soft, velvety texture. The undersurface of the leaf is densely furry and conspicuously net-veined. Flowers are greenish-yellow and borne in short, compact and sweetly scented spikes that are very attractive to insects. Fruits are conspicuously 4-winged, the wings being brittle and reddish brown. There are about 30 species of Combretum indigenous to East Africa.

Distribution: Widespread throughout eastern and southern Africa, common in dry wooded grassland, and dry *Acacia-Commiphora* bushland on shallow rocky soils. In south-central Africa, it is a common constituent also of *Brachystegia-Julbernardia* ('miombo') woodland.

Interest: The leaves and roots are used in traditional medicine for a variety of purposes that include induced abortion, as a cough remedy and the treatment of leprosy, hookworm and snakebite. The leaves are used as a dressing for wounds. The wood is termite-proof and used for implement handles and fencing posts. It produces an excellent charcoal, used locally for smelting iron. The related Cape Bush-willow (*Combretum caffrum*) is the source of combretastatin, a promising anti-cancer agent.

Fig. 16 Velvet-leaved Combretum *(Combretum molle)*

CANDELABRA TREE (*Euphorbia candelabrum*)
Mtungutungii, Mtupa (Swa.); Ol-bobongo (Maa.)

Spurge Family (*Euphorbiaceae*)

Identification: A spiny tree with ascending, candelabra-like branching from the crown. Branches are 4-5 angled, succulent and wavy, with constrictions at intervals; they produce copious sticky latex. Spines are paired and borne on separated shields. Flowers are an inconspicuous yellow-green in small clusters and fruit are 2-3 lobed, green to red. Spiny *Euphorbia* species may be confused with cacti which are native to the Americas and do not contain latex.

Distribution: Widespread in tropical Africa where it is common in thornbush country at the coast, on rocky outcrops and termite mounds in bushland, and in wooded grassland.

Interest: The latex is very toxic and is dangerous to open wounds and to the eyes: a single drop in the eye is said to cause blindness and can blister the skin of a cow. Latex has been used to make arrow poisons but it is not clear if used by itself or as a vehicle for other ingredients. Fallen trees are readily eaten by rhinos. The flowers' abundant nectar attracts bees but the honey cannot be eaten as it irritates and burns the mouth. A decoction of the pith is given to women following childbirth.

Fig. 17 Candelabra Tree *(Euphorbia candelabrum)*

KIBWEZI TREE-EUPHORBIA (*Euphorbia bussei* var. *kibwezensis*)

Spurge Family (*Euphorbiaceae*)

Identification: A tree to 12 m with winged, spiny and succulent branches which are hairless and grey-green and constricted into segments of varying shape. Flowers are borne in short clusters and are golden yellow; the 3-angled fruits are red when ripe.

Distribution: In dry bushland, often on rocky outcrops, and in dry forest fringes at the coast. Conspicuous on the descent road into Ngorongoro Crater; there is also a specimen in front of the National Museum in Nairobi. Finger or Rubber-hedge Euphorbia (*E. tirucalli*) is a shrub or small tree with cylindrical, spineless branchlets which gives its name to Manyara in Maasai who use the plant for stockades. There is a plant at the entrance to Lake Manyara National Park; and it is abundant in the Engare Sero river gorge above Lake Natron. The latex of *E. tirucalli* is toxic; the plant has been used as an insect repellant, a fish poison, in the treatment of impotence and for snakebite.

Interest: *E. bussei* is used locally for the building of grain stores.

Fig. 18 Kibwezi Tree-euphorbia (*Euphorbia bussei*)

BAOBAB (*Adansonia digitata*)
Mbuyu (Swa.); Ol-imisera (Maa.)

Baobab and Bombax Family (*Bombacaceae*)

Identification: A magestic tree with an enormously wide trunk. The bark is smooth and silvery grey and often heavily folded, and branches often remain leafless for long periods. Leaves are compound, divided into about 5-7 leaflets which are dark green and shiny. Flowers are large, waxy, white, solitary and pendulous, with a mass of fine stamens at their centre; they open at night and have an unpleasant scent which attracts fruit bats and perhaps bushbabies by which they are pollinated. Fruit are large, hard-shelled, velvety and gourd-like, and contain dark brown seeds enclosed in whitish pulp.

Distribution: Widespread and common throughout tropical Africa, in coastal bush, semi-arid savannah country and dry woodland at low altitudes. Notably abundant in Tarangire.

Interest: The leaves are used as a vegetable, the fibrous bark is used in weaving and rope-making, and the roots produce a dye. The white, powdery pulp inside the fruit contains tartaric acid and potassium bitartrate and is used for flavouring and in a refreshing drink which has been used to treat fevers. The wood is spongy and holds quantities of water, and elephants often gouge baobab trunks open with their tusks to reach the water in times of drought. Many baobabs are hollow, so serve not only as reservours of rain water but as sites of bee hives and as nesting trees for hornbills. Not surprisingly, these extraordinary trees, that are now thought to live occasionally for as long as 3000 years, are surrounded by a wealth of traditional legend the best known of which is that God planted them upside down. Baobabs are often considered sacred, and are held to have a soul, or to be possessed of the spirits of ancestors.

Fig. 19 Baobab (*Adansonia digitata*)

RED HOT-POKER TREE, or LUCKY BEAN TREE
(*Erythrina abyssinica*)
Mbamba Ngoma (Swa.); Ol-opongi (Maa.)

Pea Family (*Fabaceae, Papilionaceae,* or *Leguminosae* sub-family *Papilionoideae*)

Identification: A deciduous, flowering tree to about 12 m, with a short trunk, stout spreading branches, and a corky bark with thick spines. Leaves are trifoliolate, with broadly ovate leaflets, but the tree is usually leafless when it produces its spectacular orange-red flowers in erect heads. These are very attractive to sunbirds by which the flowers are pollinated. Fruit are furry brown pods, deeply constricted between the shiny, red and black seeds.

Distribution: Widespread in eastern and southern Africa, occurring in rocky bushland, open woodland and grassland.

Interest: Seed contain a curare-like poison which, if injected into the blood-stream, produces anaesthesia, paralysis and even death by respiratory failure. But there is said to be no danger in trading the attractive seed, which are much used as curios and in necklaces. A tonic tea is made from *Erythrina* roots and the wood is used for doors, stools and bee-hives.

Fig. 20 Red Hot-poker Tree *(Erythrina abyssinica)*

GREWIA (*Grewia bicolor*)
Mkone, Mfukufuku (Swa.), Siteti (Maa.)

Lime or Linden, and Jute Family (*Tiliaceae*)

Identification: A shrub or small tree, with oblong to lance-shaped leaves that have minutely jagged margins. The attractive flowers are yellow, borne in few-flowered clusters, appearing with the leaves. Fruit are brown, 2-lobed and sparsely hairy.

Distribution: *Grewia bicolor* is among the most widespread and common species in dry bushland, bushed grassland, and rocky places often associated with termite mounds. *Grewia* is a large genus and there are at least 27 species in our area.

Interest: The fruit are edible. Related to jute (*Corchorus capsularis*), *G. bicolor* produces a useful fibre. The wood is used in building and in making bows, arrows, spearshafts and 'rungus' (knobbed sticks).

Fig. 21 Grewia *(Grewia bicolor)*

WILD SISAL (*Sansevieria ehrenbergii*)
Oldupai (Maa.)

Sisal Family (*Agavaceae*)

Identification: A clump-forming succulent with 3-6 pairs of opposite yellowish green, spear-like, angular leaves that are almost D-shaped in cross-section. Insignificant flowers are borne in much branched heads, but flowering is rare.

Distribution: Common in many areas of dry bushland, and in grassland often around the base of kopjes, as in the Serengeti.

Interest: Wild sisal gives its name to the Olduvai Gorge, famed for discoveries of a rich array of hominid remains in the Ngorongoro Conservation Area. The plant is a local source of fibre and is a close relative of Mother-in-law's-tongue (*Sansevieria trifasciata*) which is grown as a decorative for its rosettes of stiff, fleshy leaves. Bow-string hemp comes from *Sansevieria zeylanica.* Cultivated sisal (*Agave sisalana*) which has broad, spiny tipped leaves, often becomes naturalized in lowland areas of East Africa to where it was introduced as a fibre crop from Mexico at the end of the 19th century.

Fig. 22 Wild Sisal *(Sansevieria ehrenbergii)*

TREE ALOE (*Aloe volkensii*)

Lily Family (*Liliaceae*, but now often placed in a family of their own, *Aloeaceae*)

Identification: A stout shrub or small tree, to 4 m or more tall, with an unbranched stem that is clothed with dead leaves. Leaves, which are borne in spreading terminal rosettes, are massive, toothed, succulent and olive-green; they exude a latex when cut. The decorative orange-red flowers, which are yellow at the mouth, are produced in much branched heads that attract sunbirds by which the flowers are pollinated.

Distribution: Dry, rocky bushland. Found in the Maasai Mara, Serengeti and at Olduvai Gorge, among other areas.

There are about 250 species of *Aloe*, and all are more or less succulent; some are stout herbs, others are woody. The majority are indigenous to the drier parts of eastern and southern Africa; some 60 species are native to East Africa and several of the shrubby aloes are endemic to specific areas so are rare and presumably vulnerable.

Interest: The tree aloe and its relatives are attractive plants and are commonly grown as ornamentals. Some species are heavily browsed by elephants.

The medicinal properties of *Aloe vera* have been recognized since classical times; its properties include anti-fungal, anthelmintic, bile stimulant, demulcent, purgative, styptic, sedative, tonic and wound healing actions! The leaves and sap are the plant parts used.

Fig. 23 Tree Aloe *(Aloe volkensii)*

GLORY LILY, or FLAME LILY (*Gloriosa superba*)
Mwana funzi (Swa.); Molok, molong (Maa.)

Lily Family (*Liliaceae*)

Identification: A spectacular flower which grows vigorously from a V-shaped tuber. Slender stems produce broad, lance-shaped, alternate leaves the tips of which act as tendrils, like little mobile wires for hooking themselves on to any support. The long-stalked flower is large and brilliant yellow, scarlet or dark red, each with six sharply reflexed, wavy edged petals and long protruding stamens.

Distribution: Widespread throughout tropical Africa in a range of habitats.

Interest: Much cultivated for its very attractive flowers, the glory lily has long been known to be poisonous, especially the tubers. In humans, symptoms are those of severe gastro-intestinal irritation leading to death. Various bitter principles, resins and salicylic acid have been isolated; amongst them, superbine has been shown highly toxic and as little as 0.01g is sufficient to kill a cat.

Fig. 24 Glory Lily (*Gloriosa superba*)

XEROPHYTA or STAG'S-HORN LILY
(*Xerophyta* sp.)

Vellozia Family (*Velloziaceae*)

Identification: A small shrub with much branched, fibrous 'stems' with persistent leaf-sheaths. Long, strap-shaped leaves arise in tufts at the tip of the branches. Flowers, which are borne 1-4 together on long stalks, are white to mauve. This is a strikingly attractive plant.

Distribution: In crevices on steep rocky slopes and in rock pavements in dry country. Apparently local and uncommon. *X. spekei* is known from Kenya and from Mkomazi in N. Tanzania, and other species occur further south, in Malawi, Zambia and South Africa.

Interest: The fibrous stems, which are used for cleaning metal pans and utensils, provide the plant with protection from damage during bush fires as well as with a water storage mechanism. In the dry season, the stems dry out completely but after a single shower they will absorb water and either produce new or resurrect old leaves and flowers in 3 or 4 days. For this reason, *Xerophyta* is an example of 'resurrection plants', one of the most remarkable adaptations among plants in arid zones.

Fig. 25 Xerophyta (*Xerophyta* sp.)

BEAD-BEAN (*Maerua angolensis*)

Caper Family (*Capparaceae*, or *Capparidaceae*)

Identification: A shrub or small tree with leaves variable in size and shape, usually elliptic to ovate or lanceolate and simple. Flowers are white to pale yellow green, in short terminal clusters. Petals are absent and it is the central mass of numerous, long white stamens that make the flowers showy. The fruit is like a long, slender, irregularly constricted bean pod.

There are at least 31 species of *Maerua* in East Africa. *M. triphylla*, with simple or one to three-foliolate leaves and with petals, is another of the common ones.

Distribution: Widespread in eastern and southern Africa, occurring at the coast in thickets on coral, in dry bushland, and wooded grassland.

Interest: Bead-bean wood is hard but brittle, and is used for furniture. The roots and fruit of *M. angolensis* are thought to be poisonous. *Maerua* belongs to the same family as the capers (*Capparis* spp.) several of which occur in East Africa; all are armed with two thorns at the nodes and produce berries not pods. *C. cartilaginea*, *C. fascicularis* and *C. tomentosa* are among the common species. The capers of commerce are the pickled flower buds of the Mediterranean *C. spinosa*.

Fig. 26 Bead-bean (*Maerua angolensis*)

GREY-LEAVED CORDIA (*Cordia sinensis*)
Ol-olfot, Ol-dorko (Maa.)

Forget-me-not and Heliotrope Family (*Boraginaceae*)

Identification: A shrub or small tree with slender branches tending to droop. Leaves, which are nearly opposite, are oval to oblong, greyish green and somewhat sandpapery. Flowers are cream or white, urn-shaped, and borne in terminal clusters. Fruit are ovoid, sticky and orange-red when ripe, with a conspicuous pointed tip and a saucer-like base.

Distribution: Widespread throughout eastern and southern Africa where it is common in dry bushland, bushed grassland, along river banks, and on termite mounds. Other species of *Cordia* are described on pages 138 & 140.

Interest: The fruit is edible and the wood is used for building and furniture.

Fig. 27 Grey-leaved Cordia (*Cordia sinensis*)

2. Wooded Grassland Plants

UMBRELLA THORN (*Acacia tortilis*)
Munga, Mgunga (Swa.)
Ol-gorete, Ol-tepesi, Ol-entepesi (Maa.)

Mimosa Family (*Mimosaceae*; or *Leguminosae*
sub-family *Mimosoideae*)

Identification: A medium to large tree up to
20 m, the larger ones conspicuously flat-topped and
umbrella-shaped. Leaves, like all other Acacia species,
are twice compound, sub-divided into feathery leaflets.
Florets are creamy white, borne in small round heads,
and pods are characteristically twisted into corkscrew-
like spirals. The twisted pods and the presence of two
types of thorns, hooked and straight, together make
the Umbrella Thorn immediately recognizable.

Distribution: Widespread throughout eastern and
southern Africa in a range of habitats from semi-
desert to dry bushland, along streams, and in
Acacia grassland.

Interest: The leaves and pods, which are a nutritious
fodder, are much eaten by game animals and by
livestock, and the tree can withstand heavy grazing
pressure. The gum is edible, and the bark produces
a good fibre; a bark decoction is locally used
against stomach-ache and diarrhoea. The hair roots
are used in basketry and the spreading root system
makes the tree useful in stabilizing sand. The hard
red wood is used in building, as a fuel and for
charcoal. The low, spreading branches are favoured
by the tree-climbing lions at Lake Manyara.

Fig. 28 Umbrella Thorn (*Acacia tortilis*)

WHITE-GALLED ACACIA, or WHITE THORN
(*Acacia seyal*)
Mgunga (Swa.); Oleregat, Ole-rai (Maa.)

Mimosa Family (*Mimosaceae*; or *Leguminosae* sub-family *Mimosoideae*)

Identification: A gregarious, flat-topped tree to 12 m with a distinctive bark that is powdery, pale greenish yellow to almost white. Spines are straight, in divergent pairs and leaves twice compound, with feathery leaflets. Flowers which usually appear before the leaves, are profuse, fragrant, and bright yellow, borne in large round heads. Pods are a shiny reddish brown, narrow and sickle-shaped.

Distribution: Common throughout East Africa in dry bushland and wooded grassland, often on black-cotton soils. The tree gives its name to Migunga Camp at Mto-wa-Mbu, Lake Manyara where the White-galled Acacia is common. The somewhat similar *Acacia xanthophloea* is described on p. 124, and other species of Acacia are mentioned on p. 72, 76, & 152.

Interest: The gum is edible and used to treat colds, dysentery and stomach-ache. A red dye comes from the bark which contains tannin; a tea is made from the bark.

Fig. 29 White-galled Acacia (*Acacia seyal*)

WHISTLING THORN, or BLACK-GALLED ACACIA
(*Acacia drepanolobium*)
Eluai (Maa.)

Mimosa Family (*Mimosaceae*; or *Leguminosae* sub-family *Mimosoideae*)

Identification: A shrub or small, gregarious tree to 6 m, easily recognized by the swollen black galls which form at the base of large spines, and are hollow and inhabited by ants (*Crematogaster* spp.). Creamy white flowers, that usually appear before the leaves, are borne in round heads. Pods are narrow, sickle-shaped and typically split open on the tree, the seed hanging out on thread-like stalks.

Distribution: Widespread, and locally abundant especially in seasonal swamps and black-cotton soil; also on stony ground in wooded grassland. Conspicuously common in Nairobi National Park.

Interest: Young galls, young pods and leaves are much eaten by game, especially giraffe. But the tree receives some protection by the presence of ants which act as 'askaris' (sentries) against browsers, rewarded by the secretion of sugars from extra-floral nectaries of the host tree as well as from the presence of the thorn-protected galls in which the ants raise young in safety. The whistling sound typical of this tree is caused by wind passing over the holes in galls.

The branches are used to make 'bomas' (stockades), the bark is chewed to alleviate sore throats, and a root decoction is given to mothers after delivery. The wood is hard and used for fuel and charcoal.

Fig. 30 Whistling Thorn (*Acacia drepanolobium*)

SICKLE BUSH (*Dichrostachys cinerea*)
Ol-merumuri, Enjane-ongwari (Maa.)

Mimosa Family (*Mimosaceae*; or *Leguminosae*
sub-family *Mimosoideae*)

Identification: A small, spiny, acacia-like shrub or
small tree to about 5 m tall, with flower spikes
clearly divided into two parts; one bearing long,
slender, sterile filaments that are a pale pinkish
mauve, and the other part formed by the true
flowers, like a short, compact, yellow catkin. Flower
heads droop and hang so that the pinkish part
is above the yellow, fertile section. The pods are
twisted into contorted clusters.

Distribution: Widespread throughout tropical Africa,
extending to South Africa, tropical Asia and Australia.
In our area, where it is sometimes thicket-forming,
the Sickle Bush is a typical component of *Combretum*
wooded grassland and occurs also in bushland.
Thickets are thought often to result from overgrazing,
but studies in Mkomazi Game Reserve suggest they
may be a result of fire. Thickets seem to protect
woody plants from fire until tall enough themselves
to resist a grass fire.

Interest: The wood is very hard and is used for
building, tool handles, spear-shafts and firewood.
Cattle and game eat the fruits with relish, and various
parts of the tree are used in traditional medicine: the
roots are chewed and placed on the sites of snake
bites and scorpion stings; the leaves are believed to
produce a local anaesthesia.

Fig. 31 Sickle Bush (*Dichrostachys cinerea*)

WASTE PAPER PLANT (*Cycnium tubulosum* ssp.
montanum, = *Rhamphicarpa montana*)
Kiwavi (Swa.)

Figwort Family (*Scrophulariaceae*)

Identification: A hairless erect or straggling
perennial herb from a fibrous rootstock, with linear
to lance-shaped, sparsely toothed leaves and few,
large, attractive white (ssp. *tubulosum*) or pink (ssp.
montanum) flowers on long stalks in a loose head.

Distribution: Widespread throughout eastern Africa,
south to Malawi, Mozambique and Zimbabwe,
often on black-cotton soil in grassland. It is common
at the start of the rains in the Serengeti and Maasai
Mara, looking like pieces of waste paper strewn
across the plains.

Interest: Semi-parasitic on the roots of grasses, like
its relatives *Alectra* and *Striga*, the witchweeds.

Fig. 32 Waste Paper Plant (*Cycnium tubulosum* ssp. *montanum*)

COMMICARPUS (*Commicarpus peduculatus*)

Four-O'Clock Family (*Nyctaginaceae*)

Identification: A shortly hairy, trailing and scrambling herb with oval or round leaves and striking magenta flowers borne in whorls.

Distribution: Common in thickets and riverine areas in dry grassland such as in the Ngorongoro and Loliondo Conservation Areas.

Interest: None found. Same family as the widespread ornamental *Bougainvillea*.

Fig. 33 Commicarpus (*Commicarpus peduculatus*)

YELLOW CRANE'S-BILL (*Monsonia longipes*)

Geranium Family (*Geraniaceae*)

Identification: A hairy, decumbent, much branched perennial herb, with opposite, spear-shaped leaves and attractive, pale lemon yellow (sometimes bright yellow, or white) flowers borne in heads of several flowers. Fruit are elongated and beak-like, typical of geraniums.

Distribution: Grassland and seasonally wet areas at mid-altitude, in the Rift Valley in Kenya. Common at the start of the rains in Loliondo Conservation Area. Two other species of *Monsonia* in our area.

Interest: The South African *Monsonia ovata* is known as dysentery herb because of its medicinal value. Two other species of *Monsonia* are in cultivation as decoratives in Britain.

Fig. 34 Yellow Crane's-bill (*Monsonia longipes*)

LION'S EAR (*Leonotis nepetifolia*)
Mlisha kungu (Swa.)
Ol-bibi (Maa.)

Dead-nettle, or Mint Family (*Lamiaceae*, or *Labiatae*)

Identification: A downy, erect, woody annual or short-lived perennial with long-stalked, oval leaves. The showy orange flowers, which are grouped in whorls at intervals up the 2 m tall stem, are attractive to sunbirds which pollinate them.

Distribution: Widespread and common at low altitude, as a weed of cultivation, in disturbed places, at roadsides, and around kopjes in grassland. *Leonotis mollissima*, a perennial species also with orange flowers but with leaves that are white-hairy beneath, replaces *L. nepetifolia* at altitudes above 1,950 m.

Interest: Lion's Ear is sometimes cultivated for its handsome flowers. Its roots are used locally against stomach trouble.

Fig. 35 Lion's Ear (*Leonotis nepetifolia*)

SODOM APPLE (*Solanum incanum*)
Mtunguja mwitu (Swa.)
Endulelei (Maa.)

Nightshade and Potato Family (*Solanaceae*)

Identification: An erect, felty-haired and prickly shrub to 2 m, with large oval to lance-shaped leaves often with lobed margins. Flowers borne in few-flowered heads, are mauve or purple with yellow anthers at their centre; fruit are round and blotched green, turning bright yellow when ripe.

Distribution: Common and widespread throughout tropical Africa in waste ground, on roadsides and as a weed in grassland. *Solanum* is a large, variable and difficult genus that contains the cultivated potato and aubergine. There are more than 25 species in our area.

Interest: A widely used remedy for chest troubles, ring-worm, snake-bite, earache and syphilis, the fruit pulp is used also to treat warts, bleeding wounds and toothache. The fruit juice is used locally to clot milk. Sodom Apple is frequently considered poisonous; it contains a saponin-like glycoalkaloid, solanine, which irritates the mucous membrane of the gut.

Fig. 36 Sodom Apple (*Solanum incanum*)

MORNING-GLORY (*Ipomoea mombassana*)

Morning-glory and Bindweed Family (*Convolvulaceae*)

Identification: A hairy stemmed twiner, with oval or oblong leaves and large trumpet-shaped flowers that are borne singly or in few-flowered heads; these are white, pale mauve or purple with a purple centre and a long, narrow tube.

Distribution: *I. mombassana* is a lowland species that may be common in dry bushland, *Commiphora-Combretum* woodland and seasonally flooded grassland. There are about 90 species of *Ipomoea* in East Africa where, as a group, they provide a range of bright colours to bushland, a number of different species occurring together (for instance, 15 are recorded from Mkomazi).

Interest: Several species are cultivated for their flowers, including the Common Morning-glory (*I. purpurea*) and the night-scented Moonflower (*I. alba*), but the most important member of the group is the sweet-potato (*I. batatas*), of tropical American origin and cultivated throughout the tropics.

Fig. 37 Morning-glory (*Ipomoea mombassana*)

MILKWEED (*Gomphocarpus fruticosus*)
En-daguletti (Maa.)

Milkweed Family (*Asclepiadaceae*)

Identification: A branched, upright shrub the stems of which exude milky latex when cut. Leaves are linear, their margins inrolled, and the flowers are white to yellowish green with maroon centres borne in long-stalked umbels. Fruit are large, oval, inflated bladders covered in purplish bristles.

Distribution: Widespread in dry country in grassland and along water-courses.

Interest: The plant is mildly poisonous and yields a glycoside, gofruside, that has a cardiac action. Milkweed is one of several larval food plants of the African monarch butterfly (*Danaus chrysippus*) which is unpalatable to bird predators, and is the 'model' for several African butterflies that mimic the monarch.

Fig. 38 Milkweed (*Gomphocarpus fruticosus*)

PENTANISIA (*Pentanisia ouranogyne*)
Orkelage-orger (Maa.)

Bedstraw, Madder and Coffee Family (*Rubiaceae*)

Identification: A low-growing, herbaceous perennial with linear to lance-shaped, softly hairy leaves and very attractive bright, smokey blue flowers that are borne in dense, terminal heads. Each flower has 5 petals that are joined at their base to form a tube.

Distribution: An ornamental flower of disturbed places and along roadsides in dry country, often abundant at the start of the rains throughout eastern Africa.

Interest: None.

Fig. 39 Pentanisia (*Pentanisia ouranogyne*)

HELIOTROPE (*Heliotropium undulatifolium*)

Forget-me-not and Heliotrope Family (*Boraginaceae*)

Identification: An erect, hairy herbaceous perennial, with linear, undulate leaves and short spikes of conspicuous, creamy white flowers borne on the upper side of outward-coiled branches.

Distribution: Common in the drier, medium altitude areas along roadsides and dry grassland. There are at least 13 other species in East Africa, amongst them *H. steudneri*, with oval to lance-shaped leaves, is common almost everywhere, in disturbed places and all types of bushland.

Interest: Heliotrope smells of boiled rice when driven over. It is closely related to the Peruvian Cherry-pie (*Heliotropium arborescens*) which is cultivated for its perfumed flowers.

Fig. 40 Heliotrope (*Heliotropium undulatifolium*)

CYPHOSTEMMA (*Cyphostemma orondo*)
Mwengele (Swa.)

Grape-vine Family (*Vitaceae*)

Identification: A climbing, or trailing perennial with a swollen, tuberous tap-root and large palmate leaves which are downy underneath; tendrils may or may not be present. Flowers are a rather inconspicuous greenish yellow and almost never fully open, so have a bud-like look; they are borne in branched heads up to about 30 cm (12 in) across. Fruit are berries.

Distribution: Common in bushed grassland throughout eastern Africa.

Interest: None.

Fig. 41 Cyphostemma (*Cyphostemma orondo*)

DOLICHOS (*Dolichos luticola*)

Pea Family (*Fabaceae*, *Papilionaceae*, or *Leguminosae* sub-family *Papilionoideae*).

Identification: A small herbaceous perennial with stems to 25 cm (10 in) with long, fine white hairs. The trifoliolate leaves have oval to elliptic leaflets, and flowers, which are mauve or purple, are borne in long-stalked umbel-like heads. Pods are compressed.

Distribution: On black-cotton soils in Nairobi National Park, the Ngong Hills, in Machakos and near Kajiado in Kenya and in Tanzania known from near Moshi and in Arusha Region. One of about six species of *Dolichos* in our area.

Interest: Some Dolichos species have been suspected of poisoning livestock. They are close relatives of Hyacinth bean (*Lablab purpureus*, formerly *Dolichos lablab*) which is a locally important vegetable legume, pulse and forage crop in dryland agriculture.

Fig. 42 Dolichos (*Dolichos luticola*)

VERNONIA (*Vernonia lasiopus*) Ol-euguru (Maa.)

Daisy Family (*Asteraceae*, or *Compositae*)

Identification: An erect woody perennial herb or weak shrub to 3 m, with oval to elliptic, roughly toothed leaves that have a dense mat of hairs beneath. Florets are pale mauve (or white) in cylindrical heads borne in a branched, rather flat-topped terminal cluster.

Distribution: *V. lasiopus* is widespread and common throughout eastern Africa, in disturbed ground at medium altitudes in riverine forest, *Acacia-Combretum* bushland and in bushed grassland. *Vernonia* is a vast, pan-tropical genus of about 1,000 species some 140 of which occur in East Africa.

Interest: *V. lasiopus* is used locally in Kenya against malaria, scabies and venereal disease. The pounded leaves are applied to sores to kill maggots, and the branches are used in building huts. In South Africa, an infusion of the root bark of *V. amygdalina* is used to treat bilharzia, and in Tanzania, a lethargic wild chimpanzee with diarrhoea has been reported apparently treating itself with shoot pith of *V. amygdalina*. Elsewhere various species are cultivated for their decorative flowers. In the USA, *Vernonia* is called Ironweed.

Fig. 43 Vernonia (*Vernonia lasiopus*)

BLUE MARGUERITE (*Felicia muricata*)
Olfutu (Maa.)

Daisy Family (*Asteraceae*, or *Compositae*)

Identification: A low, erect or trailing and slightly woody shrub with needle-like leaves and solitary heads, 75 mm (3 in.) across, of spreading rays which are pale to bright blue or mauve, surrounding the yellow centre.

Distribution: Locally common on clay soils in dry grassland in Maasailand, Northern Tanzania and in upland Kenya; plentiful in the Rift Valley near Naivasha, and found also in the Mara and Nairobi National Park. Common also in Loliondo.

Interest: A close relative of the South African *Felicia amelloides* which is commonly cultivated for its striking blue flower heads.

Fig. 44 Blue Marguerite (*Felicia muricata*)

BUR MARIGOLD (*Bidens schimperi*)
Kishonanguo (Swa.)

Daisy Family (*Asteraceae*, or *Compositae*)

Identification: A straggling or occasionally erect annual with finely dissected leaves and solitary, bright yellow rayed flower heads that are 4 cm (1½ in.) across.

Distribution: Widespread throughout eastern Africa southwards to Zimbabwe and Mozambique, in arable land and in dry grassland where it often forms carpets after rains. *Bidens pilosa*, the notorious weed Black Jack which is probably an introduction from tropical America, has black fruit that bear 2-4 barbed bristles that catch in clothing.

Interest: The bark fibres of Black Jack are used as twine, the leaves are used as an inferior spinach, the roots and leaves are used (in Malawi) in treatment of diarrhoea and abdominal pain, and decoctions are used (in Zimbabwe) to treat ear and eye complaints, stomach disorders and rheumatism.

Fig. 45 Bur Marigold (*Bidens schimperi*)

ASPILIA (*Aspilia mossambicensis*)

Daisy Family (*Asteraceae*, or *Compositae*)

Identification: A much branched, woody herb or shrub which, if not checked by burning, can grow to a large size and may scramble over bushes. It has rough, elliptic, lance-shaped to oval and opposite leaves and bright yellow flower heads that are solitary or borne in loose terminal clusters.

Distribution: Common and widespread in all types of bushland and bushed grassland, avoiding only the driest areas, throughout eastern and southern Africa. The very similar *A. pluriseta* is less common but equally widespread.

Interest: *Aspilia*, which is important in traditional medicine, contains high concentrations of thiarubrine A which has potent antifungal, antibacterial and antinematode properties. Chimpanzees in Tanzania have been seen using *Aspilia* apparently as a herbal medicine.

Fig. 46 Aspilia (*Aspilia mossambicensis*)

KLEINIA (*Kleinia abyssinica*)

Daisy Family (*Asteraceae*, or *Compositae*)

Identification: A tall, hairless perennial herb with ascending stems, fleshy, lance-shaped to oval leaves and nodding, bright red flower heads in loose sprays.

Distribution: Rocky places in dry bush and along stream banks. Conspicuous on the Ngorongoro Crater exit road.

Interest: None found.

Fig. 47 Kleinia (*Kleinia abyssinica*)

ANDROCYMBIUM (*Androcymbium melanthoides*)

Lily Family (*Liliaceae*)

Identification: A curious, rather charming little plant, up to 30 cm (12 in.) high from a corm with 2 or 3 narrow, grass-like stem leaves and from 2 to 6 inconspicuous greenish white flowers almost hidden by the large, papery involucre of white, green to mauve-veined bracts.

Distribution: In evergreen bushland, woodland, on rocky soils and in short grassland; often plentiful, as on the Serengeti Plains at the start of the rains. Widespread in eastern and southern Africa, from Ethiopia to Malawi and Mozambique.

Interest: Androcymbium is sometimes called Kenya Snowdrop because of its green and white flower heads. *A. europaeum* and *A. rechingeri* are rare species in the Mediterranean.

Fig. 48 Androcymbium (*Androcymbium melanthoides*)

CHLOROPHYTUM (*Chlorophytum tenuifolium*)

Lily Family (*Liliaceae*)

Identification: A large, striking plant with a fibrous rhizome with short, thick and fleshy roots bearing elliptical tubers. The lance-shaded leaves are half-folded, borne in a rosette ascending from the base; they are hairless, with margins that are often wavy. The attractive white flowers, that have strongly reflexed parts, are borne in unbranched, loose heads.

Distribution: Locally common in our area on black cotton soils and seasonally wet grassland. The plant in Fig. 49 was photographed in April near Makuyuni.

Interest: *Chlorophytum* is a large genus, with at least 56 species in East Africa. The Spider Plant, which is commonly cultivated for its decorative green and yellow foliage and heads of white flowers (that often are replaced by vegetative shoots in a viviparous reproduction) is *Chlorophytum comosum*. A closely related group of lilies belongs to *Anthericum* that differs in having small, angled seed. There are some 22 species in East Africa; *A. cooperi* is among the commoner attractive species of grasslands. St. Bernards Lily (*A. liliago*), a European species, is a cultivated ornamental.

Fig. 49 Chlorophytum (*Chlorophytum tenuifolium*)

PYJAMA LILY (*Crinum macowanii*)
Nyonyoro (Swa.)

Lily Family (*Liliaceae*; formerly separated out into *Amaryllidaceae*)

Identification: A robust, large bulbed lily with tumbled masses of long, strap-shaped bright shiny green leaves and showy, white and pink (pyjama-like), funnel-shaped flowers borne on long stalks in nodding umbels of up to 15 flowers. Blooms are often followed in a few days by large groups of rounded, inflated, crimson pods up to 5 cm in diameter.

Distribution: Widespread in upland grassland through-out Kenya and Tanzania; also from Sudan, Uganda and Ethiopia southwards to Zimbabwe.

Interest: The Pyjama Lily is an example of an 'anticipatory species', flowering shortly before the rains begin. Its large bulb ensures the plant's adaptation to savannah conditions, by storing nutrients sufficient not only to survive but also to start growth and reproduction before the onset of the rains. Combined with the flowers' strong scent, this may offer a means by which to synchronize flowering with peak populations of insect pollinators.

Fig. 50 Pyjama Lily (*Crinum macowanii*)

PARROT GLADIOLUS (*Gladiolus natalensis*)

Iris Family (*Iridaceae*)

Identification: An erect herb with leafy stems to 1.5 m. arising from a round corm that has a fibrous covering. Its large showy flowers, that vary in colour from orange to yellow, are hooded and often flecked or streaked with reddish brown. A strikingly attractive and widely familiar flower.

Distribution: A common plant in grassland that is widespread throughout eastern and southern Africa. A beautifully scented white flowered species in our area is *Gladiolus ukambanensis* which is occasionally found in rocky grassland (Fig. 52).

Interest: The Parrot Gladiolus is one of the ancestors of the ornamental cultivars of gladiolus. Some species, like the South African *G. edulis*, have edible corms that are often also dug up and eaten by baboons. Other species in East Africa include the lovely *G. watsonioides* (Fig. 101).

Fig. 52 White Gladious (*Gladious ukambanensis*)

Fig. 51 Parrot Gladiolus (*Gladiolus natalensis*)

YELLOW EULOPHIA (*Eulophia zeyheri*)

Orchid Family (*Orchidaceae*)

Identification: A beautifully showy terrestrial orchid, with large, lance-shaped, ribbed leaves that arise from the rhizome at the same time as, but separately from, the flower spike. The stout flowering shoot is up to 90 cm high and bears a dense cluster of large lemon-yellow, somewhat bell-shaped flowers at its apex, each with a deep purplish brown blotch in the throat.

Distribution: Widespread but rather local in grassland in western Kenya and northern Tanzania, including the Ngorongoro Crater, southwards to Malawi and South Africa. There are about 70 species of *Eulophia* in East Africa; many are very handsome plants and produce large colourful flowers.

E. wakefieldii, which occurs in seasonally wet grassland in Mkomazi, is one of them (Fig. 54).

Interest: *E. zeyheri* has been successfully cultivated in Kenya, despite a reputation of Eulophias being difficult to flower.

Fig. 54 Eulophia wakefieldii

Fig. 53 Yellow Eulophia (*Eulophia zeyheri*)

BONATEA (*Bonatea steudneri*)

Orchid Family (*Orchidaceae*)

Identification: A spectacular terrestrial orchid, up to 125 cm (4 ft) in height, with tuberous roots and very leafy unbranched stems. Between 6 and 30 green and white flowers are spirally arranged in loose heads one quarter of the height of the plant. At the back of the lip of each flower, there hangs an S-shaped, compressed spur 15 cm (6 in) long, making the shape of the flower somewhat insect-like.

Distribution: At roadsides, at the edge of thickets, in rocky places in bushland and grassland where it is widespread but perhaps scarce in East Africa. Known in Tanzania from the Serengeti, Ngorongoro Crater rim, in the Kilimanjaro area and the western Usambaras. Further south in Zambia, Bonatea is adapted to semi-arid mopane woodland on sandy soils in association with other xerophytic plants. Bonatea is closely related to the huge genus of the greenish Habenarias of which there are at least 113 species in East Africa.

Interest: The flowers are strongly clove-scented, so probably attractive to night-flying moths by which the orchid presumably is pollinated.

Fig. 55 Bonatea (*Bonatea steudneri*)

YELLOW-BARKED ACACIA or FEVER TREE
(*Acacia xanthophloea*)
Olerai (Maa.)

Mimosa Family (*Mimosaceae*, or *Leguminosae* subfamily *Mimosoideae*)

Identification: A tall, graceful tree to 25 m, with a characteristic, smooth, powdery, greenish yellow bark which becomes fissured in large trees. Spines are in divergent pairs, numerous in young trees. Flowers are borne in round heads, white or tinged pink (but *yellow* in southern Africa). Pods are yellowish brown, somewhat constricted between the seeds.

Distribution: Widespread in eastern and southern Africa, in groups in swampy areas, groundwater forest, beside lakes and rivers, often on black-cotton soil. Widely planted in Nairobi. Lerai Forest in Ngorongoro Crater is named after this tree.

Distribution: A fast growing ornamental with an edible gum. A bark decoction is used against indigestion. The wood is hard and makes a useful timber.

The fever tree is so-called because of its association with damp areas where mosquitoes, and therefore often also malaria, thrive. Early visitors to Africa were sure these trees were actually the cause of malaria. These impressive trees are immortalized in Rudyard Kipling's *The Elephant's Child:* "... to the banks of the great grey-green, greasy Limpopo River, all set about with fever trees".

Fig. 56 Yellow-barked Acacia (*Acacia xanthophloea*)

SYCAMORE FIG (*Ficus sycomorus*)
Mukuyu (Swa.), Orng'aboli (Maa.)

Mulberry Family (*Moraceae*)

Identification: A fine, spreading, sometimes buttressed tree to 25 m, with a distinctive yellowish bark and rounded, sandpapery leaves. Flowers are so small that several hundred fit into a tiny green ball the size of a marble; these grow in bunches directly from the trunk and main branches. Fruit, the figs, are rounded and up to 3 cm across.

Distribution: Widely distributed along rivers, often forming a distinctive part of riverine thicket, as well as in drier woodland especially where the groundwater table is high. Abundant along the Athi River in Nairobi National Park and a characteristic component of the groundwater forest at Lake Manyara.

Interest: This is the Biblical Sycamore. The wood is used for small tools and in building, and the inner part of the root produces a fibre used for weaving. An infusion of the bark and the latex are used in treatment of chest and glandular complaints. Both the leaves, which have high nutritional value, and the fruit are edible; the figs are much eaten by birds, baboon, monkeys and hyrax. There are numerous other species of *Ficus* in East Africa; the strangler fig is described on page 172. The cultivated fig is *Ficus carica*, a native of West Asia and the eastern Mediterranean, and India Rubber is *Ficus elastica*.

The Sycamore Fig has the most complex and intimate of relationships between a plant and its pollinating partners, beautifully described by David Attenborough in his *Private Life of Plants*. A female gall wasp (*Blastophaga*) lands on the fig's inflorescence and forces her way into the central chamber lined with tiny flowers. Here she unpacks pollen that she has been carrying and spreads it over the stigmas of the flowers. She then injects her eggs into the flower which reacts by developing a ball of tissue, a gall, around the wasp's egg. The female wasp dies, the grub hatches, eats the gall, pupates, then flies away.

Fig. 57 Sycamore Fig (*Ficus sycomorus*)

CAPE MAHOGANY (*Trichilia emetica*)
Mnwamaji (Swa.)

Mahogany Family (*Meliaceae*)

Identification: A handsome, evergreen tree to 20 m, with leaves made up of 4-5 opposite leaflets and a terminal leaflet, glossy above and covered in short, curly hairs underneath. The midrib of the leaflet is prominent below and extends to form a hair-like tip. Inconspicuous, greenish cream, fragrant flowers are borne in compactly branched clusters, with 5 thick petals surrounding a hairy central column of stamens. Fruit are round, stalked, velvety brown capsules that split into 3 valves, revealing the black seed each of which is attached by a thread-like stalk and enclosed in a fleshy, scarlet aril.

Distribution: Widespread in tropical Africa, in riverine forest and sites with high groundwater.

Interest: The timber is used for canoes, household utensils and for furniture, as the wood takes a good polish. The bark and roots are soaked and the liquid used as an emetic or an enema but overdoses may be lethal. The decorticated kernel is eaten by some tribes but the undecorticated seeds are said to be extremely toxic. An oil from the seed is used in making soap. The seeds themselves have a certain fascination which Keith Coates Palgrave thinks have the vacant expression of a doll's eyes!

Fig. 58 Cape Mahogany (*Trichilia emetica*)

BROAD-LEAVED CROTON (*Croton macrostachyus*)
Orkeparlu (Maa.)

Spurge Family (*Euphorbiaceae*)

Identification: A medium sized tree to 25 m with large, spreading branches and a grey trunk. Leaves are large, heart-shaped and when young covered with star-shaped hairs that give them a furry texture; they are green-grey turning orange before falling. Flowers are yellowish white, sweet-smelling and borne in long dense, erect spikes. The pea-sized fruit are grey and 2-lobed.

Distribution: Widespread in East Africa in evergreen upland forest remnants, in wooded grassland, in riverine and groundwater forest, as in Lake Manyara National Park. *Croton megalocarpus*, with narrow dark green leaves that are silvery beneath, is common in forest in Ngorongoro Conservation Area and around Nairobi. *Croton dichogamus*, a shrub or small tree 3-7 m tall, is dominant in parts of the Maasai Mara and Nairobi National Park, being most common in disturbed sites.

Interest: The wood of Broad-leaved Croton is soft and perishable but is used for making axe handles and stools. A decoction from the roots is used locally against malaria and stomach worms, the burnt leaves used as a remedy for coughs, and leaf juice improves healing of wounds. In South Africa, the bark and seeds of Fever-berry Croton (*C. megalobotrys*) are reputed to be effective both as a cure and prophylactic against malaria.

Fig. 59 Broad-leaved Croton (*Croton macrostachyus*)

RAUVOLFIA, or QUININE TREE (*Rauvolfia caffra*)
Olemudongo (Maa.)

Periwinkle and Oleander Family (*Apocynaceae*)

Identification: An evergreen shrub or tree to 20 m with a dense, rounded crown and long, leathery lance-shaped leaves borne in whorls of 3-5 on short, grooved stalks. The ornamental flowers are white, sweetly scented but very small, in spreading branched heads. Fruit are round, 2-lobed and fleshy, turning black when mature; they are relished by birds.

Distribution: Widespread in eastern and southern Africa, almost invariably found along watercourses in riverine forest and in sites with available ground water, as in Lake Manyara National Park in Tanzania. Common in Meru district and the Kedong Valley in Kenya.

Interest: All parts of the plant contain a thin, bitter latex that was once thought a cure for malaria by now known to be ineffective. The root bark contains reserpine, an alkaloid used as a tranquilliser in the treatment of high blood pressure. Commercially, reserpine is obtained from related species, *Rauvolfia serpentina* and *R. vomitoria*.

Fig. 60 Rauvolfia (*Rauvolfia caffra*)

WILD MANGO, or FOREST TOAD TREE
(*Tabernaemontana ventricosa*)

Periwinkle and Oleander Family (*Apocynaceae*)

Identification: A leafy, evergreen shrub or small tree to 10 m, with glossy dark green elliptic leaves and showy, sweetly scented white to cream flowers borne in dense heads. Fruit are paired, rounded and ridged, splitting when mature to expose bright orange pulp containing many brown seeds. All parts of the plant contain copious milky latex.

Distribution: Widespread in eastern and southern Africa in riverine and groundwater forest, as in Lake Manyara National Park where it is very abundant; also in evergreen forest further south. *T. stapfiana*, with much larger fruit and flowers that resemble Frangipani, occurs in East Africa in upland forest around Mt. Kenya and at Kericho and Limuru.

Interest: Some species of *Tabernaemontana* like *T. citrifolia* are planted for ornament. The shrivelled, gaping fruit of *T. elegans* (Mbombo in Swahili) are said to resemble a toad's head. Its edible pulp is relished by birds, monkeys and baboons; the coagulated latex is used as a styptic and the root is a remedy for pulmonary disease. The latex of the Asian *T. malaccensis* has been used as an arrow poison in Malaysia.

Despite its common name, *Tabernaemontana* is not closely related to the true mango (*Mangifera indica*).

Fig. 61 Wild Mango (*Tabernaemontana ventricosa*)

TOOTHBRUSH TREE, or MUSTARD TREE
(*Salvadora persica*)
Mswaki (Swa.), Eremit (Maa.)

Mustard Tree Family (*Salvadoraceae*)

Identification: A scrambling shrub or small evergreen tree, often with hanging branches. Leaves are elliptic and somewhat fleshy, and flowers are tiny, greenish cream borne in loose, slender branched sprays. Fruit are round and fleshy, translucent white to pink or red.

Distribution: Widespread and common in dry acacia bushland, wooded grassland and, especially, along rivers and luggas. The Toothbrush Tree, which can become thicket forming, is often found on termite mounds.

Interest: Fruit are edible and have a sweet, aromatic or peppery taste. Branchlets are used as toothbrushes in East Africa; roots are used for cleaning teeth and to relieve toothache in southern Africa.

Fig. 62 Toothbrush Tree (*Salvadora persica*)

LARGE-LEAVED CORDIA (*Cordia africana*)

Forget-me-not and Heliotrope Family (*Boraginaceae*)

Identification: An attractive forest tree to 10 m or more tall with a rounded crown and an often crooked trunk, eye-catching and handsome in flower. Leaves are large, broadly oval, leathery and rough to the touch above. The showy flowers are white, funnel-shaped, sweetly scented and with crinkly petals, borne in dense terminal heads. Fruit are round, fleshy, and yellowish, about 1 cm diameter, each held in a hairy cup, and contain seed embedded in sticky, sweet flesh.

Distribution: Widespread in wooded grassland, forest and along river banks from Ethiopia southwards to Zimbabwe. In Kenya, common in Kakamega and Meru Forests. In Tanzania, in groundwater forest in Lake Manyara National Park and planted for ornament in Arusha. *Cordia* is a large pan-tropical genus of trees and shrubs. The exotic Geiger-tree (*C. sebestena*) from tropical America is widely cultivated for its attractive orange or red flowers. Other common species indigenous to East Africa include the Sandpaper Cordia or Msasa (*C. monoica*) which gives its name to Msasa River at Lake Manyara, Grey-leaved Cordia (*C. sinensis*; p. 70) and Blue-bark Cordia (*C. goetzei*; p. 140).

Interest: The wood of Large-leaved Cordia, which has edible fruit, is used in furniture making; it works easily and polishes well. It is also used for making bee-hives which are often hung in its branches, as its nectar is very attractive to bees. The fruit gum is used as glue. It is also a good shade tree; leaf fall in the dry season can be heavy but makes good mulch.

Fig. 63 Large-leaved Cordia (*Cordia africana*)

BLUE-BARK CORDIA, or RHINO RIB
(*Cordia goetzei*)

Forget-me-not and Heliotrope Family
(*Boraginaceae*)

Identification: A shrub to small tree with a distinctive square trunk that is strongly ridged, and with blue-grey bark that flakes to reveal the paler dove-grey to yellowish green underbark. Leaves are oval to elliptic. Funnel-shaped, creamy white flowers are borne on slender stalks in loose heads; fruits are like small, sharply pointed acorns partly enclosed in basal cups.

Distribution: Widespread but local, from the Kenya Coast to Mkomazi and Lake Manyara in Tanzania, southwards to Zimbabwe, in riverine habitats and in groundwater forest; also in coastal forest on coral. Sometimes on termite mounds, hot rocky slopes and in dry river valleys. There are fine specimens in groundwater forest in Lake Manyara National Park. Other *Cordia* species are described on p. 70 & 138.

Interest: None.

Fig. 64 Blue-bark Cordia (*Cordia goetzei*)

AFRICAN TULIP TREE, NANDI FLAME, or FLAME OF THE FOREST
(*Spathodea campanulata*)
Kibobakasi (Swa.)

Jacaranda and Bignonia Family (*Bignoniaceae*)

Identification: A very handsome deciduous flowering tree with a rounded crown to 18 m and large, compound leaves of 9-13 leaflets that are velvety beneath. Flowers are trumpet-shaped, bright orange-scarlet with a yellow margin and throat, borne in dense terminal clusters. Flower buds, which are densely covered in soft brown hairs, contain copious secreted water that squirts out when buds are squeezed or pierced, giving it the name 'Fountain Tree'. Fruit are oblong, black woody capsules containing winged seed.

Distribution: In fringing and riverine forest in western Kenya, Uganda and the Congo but now very widely planted for ornament, often in avenues, like its relative the Brazilian Jacaranda (*J. mimosifolia*), with striking mauve-blue flowers.

Immortalized in Elspeth Huxley's *The Flame Trees of Thika*, the African Tulip Tree is one of the most attractive trees indigenous to East Africa where it is often planted as a shade tree in coffee estates, as in Arusha. The scarlet flowers are also attractive to sunbirds by which they are pollinated.

Bird pollinated flowers are often red and lack perfume: insects are largely insensitive to the red end of the spectrum so that red was available for advertising to birds which nevertheless lack a sense of smell.

Interest: An infusion of the bark is used locally against liver complaints; the wood is brownish white, very soft and light.

Fig. 65 African Tulip Tree (*Spathodea campanulata*)

SAUSAGE TREE (*Kigelia africana*)
Mwegea (Swa.), *Ol-sunguroi*, *Ol-darpoi* (Maa.)

Jacaranda and Bignonia Family (*Bignoniaceae*)

Identification: A low-branched tree with a rounded crown to 9 m in open woodland but much taller in riverine fringes. Leaves, which are very rough to the touch, are compound consisting of 3-5 pairs plus a terminal leaflet. The spectacular flowers have crumpled, dark maroon petals, each flower like an upturned trumpet hanging in loose heads on long rope-like stalks. Their smell is unpleasant but attracts fruit bats by which they are pollinated at night. It is thought that isolation of flowers on long stalks below the canopy assist their location by bats which rely on echoes of their ultrasonic squeaks in navigation. The fruit are very unusual, like huge grey sausages up to 1 m long weighing as much as 10 kg and containing fibrous pulp in which the seed are embedded.

Distribution: Widespread throughout tropical Africa, in wooded grassland, forest margins and riverine forest.

Interest: Fallen flowers are eaten by game and livestock. Unripe fruit are said to be poisonous but are used as a remedy for syphilis and rheumatism. Ripe fruit, which are eaten occasionally by giraffe, are dried, baked and sliced to ferment beer. The seed are also sometimes roasted and eaten, or placed in beer but, if left too long, can make it poisonous. It is also used in beer to enlarge the sexual organs. The powdered fruit is used as a dressing for ulcers and to increase lactation, among a range of other medical uses. The wood is rather soft but tough and has been used for making canoes.

Fig. 66 Sausage Tree (*Kigelia africana*)

WILD DATE PALM (*Phoenix reclinata*)
Mkindu (Swa.), Ol-tukai (Maa.)

Palm Family (*Arecaceae*, or *Palmae*)

Identification: A slender palm to 10 m, sometimes bent over, with persistent leaf bases near the top. The large compound leaves, up to 3 m long, made up of many leaflets give a feathery appearance. Male and female flowers are borne on different trees: male ones are creamy brown and the smaller female ones are greenish. Fruit are yellow-brown to dull red.

Distribution: Gregarious along watercourses and beside swamps in the lowlands, on rocky hillsides in upland areas and in disturbed forest. Abundant in groundwater forest at Lake Manyara, and striking in the Engare Sero River gorges south of Lake Natron.

Phoenix dactylifera, native to the Middle East, is the Date Palm of commerce, *P. canariensis* from the Canary Islands is a widely grown ornamental palm sometimes cultivated in upland Kenya, and *P. sylvestris*, indigenous to India, produces a sugar from which jaggery, palm wine and arrack are made.

Interest: The leaf fibre of the Wild Date Palm is used for weaving, basketry and house building and the roots yield a dye. The fruit is edible.

There are various legends connecting the tree with the phoenix, the mythical bird, "of gorgeous plumage, fabled to be the only one of its kind, and to live to 600 years in the Arabian desert, after which it burnt itself to ashes on a funeral pyre of aromatic twigs ignited by the sun and fanned by its own wings, only to emerge from its ashes with renewed youth, to live through another cycle of years". One theory was that the Phoenicians gave the name *Phoenix* to the palm in the belief that when the tree is burnt down to the root, it rises again fairer than ever!

Fig. 67 Wild Date Palm (*Phoenix reclinata*)

BORASSUS PALM, or AFRICAN FAN PALM
(*Borassus aethiopum*)
Mvumo, Mtappa, Mchapa (Swa.)

Palm Family (*Arecaceae*, or *Palmae*)

Identification: A palm tree to 25 m with a straight grey trunk. Young stems are clad with persistent dead leaves; older ones have a swelling above the middle. Leaves are very large and fan-shaped, deeply divided into numerous segments. Male flower heads, which are borne on different trees from female ones, are large branched catkins about 1.5 m long; female inflorescences are longer but unbranched. Fruit are large, orange-brown, round and shiny, containing 3 seed embedded in fibrous pulp.

Distribution: Widespread, in coastal woodland, along rivers and in grassland where the water-table is high, from Uganda and Kenya southwards to South Africa. The Doum Palm, or Mkoma (*Hyphaene compressa*), is an unusual branched palm that is also found at the coast and along seasonal water-courses in East Africa.

Interest: The fruit, which is much liked by elephant, is edible and the sap is made into an excellent palm wine. Leaves are used in weaving baskets and mats, and the stem yields a type of starch. The wood is hard, heavy and resistant to termites and is used for dug-out canoes; in some areas, the swollen stem is hollowed out for food storage. The seed of the Doum Palm is used as"vegetable ivory", like the tropical American Ivory-nut Palm (*Phytelephas macrocarpa*), once used for turning into buttons and billiard balls.

Fig. 68 Borassus Palm (*Borassus aethiopum*)

GREAT SEDGE (*Cyperus immensus*)

Sedge Family (*Cyperaceae*)

Identification: Huge, robust evergreen, 3-angled stems bear grass-like leaves and leaf-like bracts that surround a branched umbel of numerous flower spikes, with flowers arranged in two opposite ranks.

Distribution: In seasonally inundated grassland, temporary water-holes and in swampy glades in forest where the water-table is too high for successful growth of trees. In Lake Manyara National Park, Great Sedge forms dense tussocks where flooding by fresh water is prolonged. Found occasionally also in Mkomazi. *Cyperus involucratus* and *C. longus* are each found in marginal areas on somewhat drier ground in similar places.

Interest: Great sedge, often incorrectly referred to as a reed, is a close relative of Papyrus (*Cyperus papyrus*) the pithy stems of which produced the paper of the Egyptians. Chufa, or Yellow Nut-grass (*Cyperus esculentus*) produces edible tubers, and several sedges including both *C. involucratus* and *C. longus* (Sweet Galingale) are cultivated as ornamentals. In the USA, Galingale is also used for basket making.

Fig. 69 Great Sedge (*Cyperus immensus*)

RED THORN (*Acacia lahai*)
Oldebesi, Oltepessi (Maa.)

Mimosa Family (*Mimosaceae*; or *Leguminosae* sub-family *Mimosoideae*)

Identification: A flat-topped tree to 15 m, with dark brown, rough bark and straight, pale spines in pairs. The flowers borne in spikes, are white, cream or pale yellow and pods are broad, straight or curved and shiny brown, splitting on the tree to liberate the round, flat seeds.

Distribution: Locally common where upland forest has disappeared, forming dense woodland or invading grassland, usually indicating effects of fire. Common in the Rift Valley near Kericho in Kenya, and conspicuous on the rim and northern wall of Ngorongoro Crater where locally it forms woodland.

Interest: The wood is red and very hard, heavy and durable and is used in construction work. The bark, which is fire resistant and protects the young tree from burning, is used locally as an astringent.

Fig. 70 Red Thorn (*Acacia lahai*)

SAND OLIVE (*Dodonaea angustifolia*)
Mkaa Pwani (Swa.), Orgeturai, Ol-tuyesi (Maa.)

Soapberry and Litchi Family (*Sapindaceae*)

Identification: A thin stemmed shrub or small tree, usually 2-4 m tall, with resinous, rusty red branchlets. Leaves are thin, narrow, glossy and sticky when young. Flowers are small and yellow-green, grouped in short, dense terminal heads. Fruits are distinctive capsules, greenish red with 2-3 papery wings in masses that look like bunches of flowers.

Distribution: In evergreen bushland in rocky, stony and sandy places and on lava soils; it is also a pioneer in forest margins, as for instance at the foot of Mt. Meru at Momela Gate to Arusha National Park where it is dominant. The Sand Olive at the coast is *Dodonuea viscosa*. Despite their name, they are not true olives like Loliondo (*Olea cupensis*) and Wild Olive (*Olea europaea* ssp. *africana*) both of which are components of upland evergreen forest in our area.

Interest: The wood is hard and heavy and is used for tool handles. An infusion from roots has long been regarded as a reliable remedy for the common cold, and a decoction of the leaves is a mild purgative and a treatment for rheumatism and haemorrhoids. Sand Olive is a quick growing hedge plant that stabilizes sand and withstands fire to an amazing degree.

Fig. 71 Sand Olive (*Dodonaea angustifolia*)

AFRICAN PENCIL CEDAR (*Juniperus procera*)
Ol-tarakwa (Maa.)

Cypress Family (*Cupressaceae*)

Identification: A large evergreen conifer to 40 m, with a straight trunk and pyramidal shape when young, then spreading to form a high, irregular crown. The pale brown bark is typically fissured vertically, cracking and peeling in long strips. Leaves are of two kinds: juvenile leaves are needle-like and spreading; on adult plants, they are scale-like and appressed to the branches. Male cones are yellowish, rounded and very small whereas female cones, borne on a separate tree, are fleshy and berry-like covered in a waxy bluish bloom and contain 1-4 hard seed in green pulp.

Distribution: Common on the slopes of Mt. Kenya, the escarpment between Limuru and Naivasha, on Kilimanjaro and Mt. Meru. From Kenya and Uganda southwards to Zimbabwe in highland forest and forest remnants, and on shallow rocky soils, in pure stands or in association with Podo (p. 160), Broad-leaved Croton (p. 130) or Wild Olive. The more southerly Mulanje Cedar is the related *Widdringtonia nodiflora*. Neither are true cedars (species of *Cedrus* in the Pine Family); 'cedar' is used loosely for various trees with characteristically fragrant wood.

Interest: The wood of African Pencil Cedar is of major importance in Kenya for building, joinery, roofing and fencing; it is hard, durable, termite resistant and fine grained. It was once exported for the manufacture of pencils (like *Juniperus virginiana*, Eastern Red Cedar, which is grown commercially in the USA for this purpose). Bark is used for bee-hives. The aromatic resin makes the tree very susceptible to fire. Oil of Juniper is obtained from the European *Juniperus communis* and gives the essential flavour to gin (it also has an ancient reputation as an abortifacient); the medicinal Oil of Cade comes from the Mediterranean *J. oxycedrus*

Fig. 72 African Pencil Cedar (*Juniperus procera*)

AERANGIS (*Aerangis thomsonii*)

Orchid Family (*Orchidaceae*)

Identification: Stem stout and woody, up to 60 cm long, bearing aerial roots. Leaves are hard, leathery and deep green, with tips that are characteristically unequally bilobed. Flowers are strikingly beautiful: pure white, each with a long (100-150 mm) tubular spur, usually 6-12 flowers to an inflorescence and two flower spikes per plant. Flowers, the parts of which are strongly reflexed, are sweetly scented especially after dark.

Distribution: Widespread as an epiphyte, especially on African Pencil Cedar, in montane forest at altitudes above 2,135 m (7,000 feet). There are about 20 species of *Aerangis* in East Africa.

Interest: A beautiful orchid that has been brought into cultivation.

Fig. 73 Aerangis (*Aerangis thomsonii*)

PODO, or EAST AFRICAN YELLOW-WOOD
(*Podocarpus latifolius*)
Ol-biribiri (Maa.)

Podo, or Yellow-wood Family (*Podocarpaceae*)

Identification: An evergreen coniferous tree to 30 m with a large, buttressed trunk and greyish brown bark that peels in long strips, giving a ragged appearance. The aromatic leaves are large (up to 15 cm long) linear, spirally arranged and crowded towards the ends of branches, with juvenile leaves much larger than mature leaves. Male and female trees are separate. Male cones are pinkish, like hanging catkins; female cones are berry-like, borne on a swollen fleshy, red receptacle.

Podocarpus falcatus differs in its smaller leaves, and unswollen fruit receptacles.

Distribution: Widespread in upland rain forest, from Uganda and Kenya southwards to South Africa, *P. latifolius* preferring wetter zones than does *P. falcatus*. Either species can be locally dominant, forming almost pure stands; also often associated with African Pencil Cedar (p. 156).

Interest: Podo is an important and high quality softwood. The timber is a uniform, pale yellow colour; it seasons and saws well, and takes a good finish. Podo has been much used in internal carpentry, in flooring and as a source of plywood. A bark decoction is used as a remedy for stomach ache, and the fruit are much liked by monkeys and hornbills.

Fig. 74 Podo (*Podocarpus latifolius*)

NUXIA, or BRITTLE WOOD (*Nuxia congesta*)
Ol-burin (Maa.)

Strychnos Family (*Loganiaceae*)

Identification: A much branched tree to 10 m or more, with a fluted trunk, pale greyish brown flaking bark, and low, drooping branches. Leaves are oval, borne in threes at the end of branches. Flowers are white and fragrant, in dense congested, flat-topped heads at the end of branchlets; fruit are small hairy capsules.

Distribution: Widespread, from Uganda and Kenya southwards to South Africa, locally common in montane forest and forest margins, on hilltops above the forest margin and in the bamboo zone.

Interest: The wood is white and soft and is used for fuel and building. Nuxia is related to *Strychnos*, a genus with numerous species indigenous to Africa. Strychnine is extracted from the Indian *S. nux-vomica* and *S. toxifera* produces one of the constituents of curare, used in South America as an arrow poison by causing progressive paralysis and eventual heart failure.

Fig. 75 Nuxia (*Nuxia congesta*)

CAPE CHESTNUT (*Calodendrum capense*)
Ol-larashi (Maa.)

Citrus and Rue Family (*Rutaceae*)

Identification: A spectacularly beautiful, deciduous flowering tree to 20 m, with a shapely spreading crown. Leaves are simple, broadly oval, opposite and short-stalked. Flowers are large, showy and pink, each with 5 long and narrow petals which alternate with 5 sterile stamens that are pale pink dotted with maroon glands. Fruit are knobbly, round and 5-lobed, splitting open to reveal the shiny black seeds.

Distribution: Widespread in riverine forest and in upland forest remnants from Kenya southwards to South Africa. It is a conspicuous component of the forest along the Rift Valley Escarpment in Kenya as well as on the Ngorongoro Crater ascent road in Tanzania. Cape Chestnut is also much planted as an ornamental.

Interest: The bitter-flavoured seed yield an oil used in making soap. The timber is tough, bends well and is used in building, in making furniture like stools and for implements. Much used for lining avenues for its decorative flowers.

Fig. 76 Cape Chestnut (*Calodendrum capense*)

PILLAR-WOOD, or ONION-WOOD
(*Cassipourea malosana*)
Oliami-orok, Ol-lorget (Maa.)

Mangrove Family (*Rhizophoraceae*)

Identification: A tall evergreen tree to 25 m or more in height with a straight, smooth, silvery pillar-like trunk crowned with a pedestal of dark green broadly oval leaves that have somewhat toothed margins. Flowers are greenish white and borne in the axils; fruit are small oval capsules.

Distribution: A typical component of the montane high forest, conspicuous along the road to Ngorongoro Crater. Also found on Mt. Kenya and the Aberdares, in drier forest with Podo, Pencil Cedar and Olive, in understory in moister forest, and in forest remnants. One of six species of *Cassipourea* in Kenya. Among the related mangroves, the association of plants of the muddy swamps at the mouths of rivers and elsewhere in the tropics, Red Mangrove (*Rhizophora mucronata*) is one of the commonest.

Interest: The timber of Pillar-wood is valued for its strength and was used in the construction of Crater Lodge in Ngorongoro. The wood is both hard and elastic but is liable to attack by borers.

Fig. 77 Pillar-wood (*Cassipourea malosana*)

SPINY TREE FERN (*Cyathea manniana*)

Tree Fern Family (*Cyatheaceae*)

Identification: An evergreen fern with a straight stem to 10 m covered with brown scales and old persistent leaf bases. Fronds, which arch from the crown, are large and compound, and their stems are sharply spiny. The presence of prickles on leaf bases and stalks distinguishes this species from other tree ferns in eastern and southern Africa.

Distribution: A widespread tree fern, from West Africa extending eastwards to the Rwenzori Mountains and the 'Impenetrable Forest' in Kigezi in Uganda. In Kenya, the Spiny Tree Fern occurs in moist evergreen forest along streams and in valleys, sometimes in more open forest remnants, distributed southwards in suitable montane habitats in Tanzania to the eastern highlands of Zimbabwe. On Mt. Kenya, where the much smaller *Cyathea humilis* also occurs, the Spiny Tree Fern is often associated with the fern *Asplenium hypomelas* which grows as an epiphyte in the leaf scars and on the ground at its base.

Interest: The pulpy pith of some tree ferns is occasionally eaten. Several species of *Cyathea* are cultivated for their attractive foliage but they are frost-tender and need a humid atmosphere.

Fig. 78 Spiny Tree Fern (*Cyathea manniana*)

WILD BANANA (*Ensete ventricosum*)
Ol-musalala (Maa.)

Banana Family (*Musaceae*)

Identification: An herbaceous tree to 4 m tall with an unbranched false stem made of old, overlapping leaf sheaths. The leaves themselves are oblong and huge, to 5 m long and 1m wide; they are spirally arranged and almost stalkless, with a midrib that is often rose-pink. Flowers are borne in massive pendulous spikes up to 3 m long, protected by large maroon bracts; fruit are leathery and resemble a 'hand' of small bananas each containing a mass of hard, pea sized seed.

Distribution: Widespread throughout eastern and southern Africa in high rainfall forest, forested ravines and along rivers.

Interest: Used as a staple food crop in parts of Ethiopia where a meal is prepared from the fresh or fermented pulp in the stem and roots. A strong, fine fibre is obtained from leaf bases, used for cordage and sacking; the leaves are used for thatching. The plant is also an outstanding ornamental for frost-free areas. The cultivated banana and plantains belong to the related *Musa paradisiaca*, *M. acuminata* and their varieties, and Manila Hemp or Abaca is obtained from *M. textilis.*

Fig. 79 Wild Banana (*Ensete ventricosum*)

STRANGLER FIG (*Ficus thonningii*)
Mugumu; Oreteti (Maa.)

Mulberry Family (*Moraceae*)

Identification: A large tree to 20 m, often multi-stemmed from the growth of aerial roots, sometimes epiphytic and often a strangler. The bark is smooth and grey, and the leaves are generally oval but vary greatly in both shape and size. Figs are small, rounded, and borne on very short stalks in clusters in the axils of terminal branches; they may be smooth or warty and either yellow or crimson when ripe.

Distribution: Widespread in a variety of habitats, from wooded grassland, in riverine sites, to upland forest. Common around Nairobi. In Tanzania, there is a particularly well-known specimen on the slopes of Mt. Meru, the Fig Tree Arch in Arusha National Park. This unusual tree formation has been caused by the strangling habit of this fig: seed were once dropped in the fork of a host tree by a feeding bird. Following germination, aerial roots are put out, eventually reaching the ground. There they dig into the soil and the plant now grows more vigorously. Other roots begin to wrap themselves around the trunk of their host, slowly strangling it. In the case of the Fig Tree Arch, there must have been not one but two host trees, which once stood on either side of the track. Aerial roots in the centre of the arch are browsed off by elephants, so keeping the arch open.

The Strangler Fig is an important ceremonial meeting tree, widely regarded as the sacred home of ancestral spirits.

Interest: The edible figs are much favoured by birds, small mammals and monkeys, fibre from the bark is used for string, and branches are used as firesticks. Among the 30 or so species of fig in eastern Africa, Fig is described on p. 126. Asian figs include the huge Banyan (*Ficus benghalensis*) and the Weeping Fig (*F. benjamina*) that is an ornamental and widely planted street tree in Arusha and Nairobi.

Fig. 80 Strangler Fig (*Ficus thonningii*)

PINK BALSAM, or JEWEL-WEED
(Impatiens pseudoviola)

Balsam Family *(Balsaminaceae)*

Identification: An annual or short-lived herbaceous perennial to 40 cm tall, with erect, fleshy, branched stems that are usually hairless. The flimsy leaves are more-or-less spirally arranged and the flowers, which are either single or in a loose head of 2 or 3, are large spurred, and violet pink in colour with a crimson, or sometimes yellow, blotch toward the base of the joined petals. Seed are borne in an explosive capsule which gives balsams the name 'touch-me not'.

Distribution: In damp shady places beside streams, and on tree stumps, in moist upland forests in central and southern Kenya, and on both Mt. Kilimanjaro and Mt. Meru in northern Tanzania. There are more than 100 species of balsam in Africa and about 70 occur in East Africa. The Uluguru Mountains above Morogoro in Tanzania are a centre of particular diversity.

Interest: *Impatiens pseudoviola* is cultivated in Europe for its attractive flowers. The well-known Buzy Lizzie is *I. walleriana*, widely grown as an ornamental pot plant. The Garden Balsam of the USA is *I. balsamina*, which is of Asian origin. Himalayan Balsam (*I. glandulifera*) has become naturalized both in North America and in Europe where it has become a noxious weed along river banks.

Fig. 81 Pink Balsam (*Impatiens pseudoviola*)

KILIMANJARO BALSAM, or JEWEL-WEED
(*Impatiens kilimanjari*)

Balsam Family (*Balsaminaceae*)

Identification: This balsam differs from the Pink Balsam (p. 174) in having large striking flowers that are bright orange, or bicoloured scarlet with a long, curved spur that is bright yellow. Leaves have jagged, serrate margins.

Distribution: Endemic to Mt. Kilimanjaro where it is frequent in the montane rain forest. The dark red or scarlet balsam that is found in wet highland forest and in the bamboo zone on Mt. Kenya and the Aberdares is *I. fischeri.*

Interest: Balsams are restricted to wet and shady places beside streams, in moist forests and on wet mountains, habitats which are themselves inherently patchy in Africa. Their intrinsic variability coupled with their poor capacity to disperse together account for the extent to which particular species of balsam have become adapted to very localized conditions, including their pollinators. Balsams offer their pollinators nectar in a sac (spur) and attract them with brightly coloured flowers. Whether a bee, butterfly or bird is the most effective pollinator depends on the exact shape and arrangement of the flower. Congo Cockatoo (*I. niamniamensis*) is an example of a bird-pollinated species.

Fig. 82 Kilimanjaro Balsam (*Impatiens kilimanjari*)

STREPTOCARPUS, or CAPE PRIMROSE
(*Streptocarpus glandulosissimus*)

African Violet and Gloxinia Family (*Gesneriaceae*)

Identification: A softy hairy, trailing or semi-erect perennial herb with fleshy stems bearing stalked leaves and loose heads of large, showy violet and purple flowers with conspicuous lower lips.

Distribution: In shady, wet upland forest and stream sides.

Some 21 species in East Africa. More common in Tanzania than in Kenya.

Interest: Numerous species of *Streptocarpus* including *S. glandulosissimus* are widely grown as ornamentals for their showy flowers. Unusual among dicotyledons, some have only a single enlarged seed-leaf that develops at the expense of the second one.

Closely related to the African Violet (*Saintpaulia*) which has a very restricted distribution in the wild in Tanzania.

Fig. 83 Streptocarpus (*Streptocarpus glandulosissimus*)

MEXICAN FLEABANE (*Erigeron karvinskianus*)

Daisy Family (*Compositae, or Asteraceae*)

Identification: A spreading, branched perennial to 45 cm tall, with slender stems and almost unstalked leaves the lower of which are 3-lobed. The small flower heads are daisy-like and borne terminally on branches, with white or pink ray florets.

Distribution: Widespread throughout highland East Africa; conspicuous on Ngorongoro Crater Rim where Fig. 55 was taken. An introduced weedy species, from Mexico and Central America.

Interest: Mexican Fleabane is widely naturalized especially on walls throughout Europe where it is cultivated for its attractive flowers. In Britain it has received the Award of Garden Merit from the Royal Horticultural Society. Alpine Fleabane (*Erigeron alpinus*) is native to the European Alps.

Fig. 84 Mexican Fleabane (*Erigeron karvinskianus*)

FIRE-BALL LILY (*Scadoxus multiflorus*)
Osila (Maa.)

Lily Family (*Liliaceae*; formerly placed in *Amaryllidaceae*)

Identification: A magnificent bulbous plant, with about 150 narrow petalled red flowers borne in a tight ball on stout stalks that appear with the first rains, before the leaves, looking like a giant shaving brush. The broadly lance-shaped basal leaves are thick and upright, with purple-spotted sheaths. The similar Pom-pom Lily (*Boophane disticha*) differs in having its leaves arranged in a fan.

Distribution: Widespread in a range of habitats throughout tropical Africa, in rocky places in semi-arid areas, open grassland, and both riverine and upland forest. The Scarlet Mop-head Lily (*Scadoxus cyrtanthiflorus*) is a spectacular relative with a more restricted distribution; it is found in forest in the Rwenzori Mountains.

Interest: Formerly placed in the genus *Haemanthus* meaning 'blood-red flowers', the Fire-ball Lily is cultivated in frost-free areas for its showy flowers.

Fig. 85 Fire-Ball Lily (*Scadoxus multiflorus*)

STAIRS' DISA (*Disa stairsii*)

Orchid Family (*Orchidaceae*)

Identification: A terrestrial or rarely epiphytic orchid, with hairy roots without tubers and a single stem arising from a basal rosette of long, pointed leaves. The robust inflorescence is a dense conical spike borne on a leafy stem of very handsome flowers that are pink, deep rose-purple or burgundy. Individual flowers have erect, dorsal sepals that are hooded, a curved spur at their base, and a strap-shaped lip.

Distribution: Widespread and sometimes locally abundant in moorland, and in glades at the upper limits of montane forest, in bamboo and in the *Hagenia-Hypericum* zones on mountains throughout East Africa, from the Rwenzori Mountains and Virunga Volcanoes eastwards to Mt. Elgon, the Aberdares and Mt. Kenya, south to Mt. Meru, Kilimanjaro and the Ulugurus.

Interest: Named after Leutenant Stairs, a member of the Stanley Expedition in 1889, this is one of a group of about 130 species of the most handsome and colourful ground orchids in Africa, predominantly South African but with 27 species in East Africa. Unfortunately, *Disa* species have proved difficult to cultivate.

Fig. 86 Stairs' Disa (*Disa stairsii*)

MOUNTAIN BAMBOO (*Arundinaria alpina*)
Mwanzi (Swa.), Ol-diani (Maa.)

Grass Family (*Gramineae, or Poaceae*)

Identification: Unmistakable: the most tree-like grass, with yellowish green, hollow, woody stems to about 15 m that are thickened at the nodes. The leaves are narrowly elliptic and pointed. Flowering and fruiting, which occurs in patches, is followed by plant death.

Distribution: Bamboo forms a zone below the *Hagenia-Hypericum* belt and above the montane forest, at about 2,400-3,000 m, on moist slopes of all the East African mountains, with the notable exception of Kilimanjaro on which bamboo occurs only in a few small patches on its northern slopes. In some situations, bamboo can form an almost impenetrable barrier.

Interest: The uses of bamboo are legion, from fencing and in construction to uses in fishing, as a fibre source in paper making and as musical instruments. Split bamboo is used in basketry and in piping. Young shoots are an important human food in Asia, and in the Virunga Volcanoes, the tender white shoots of Mountain Bamboo make up the bulk of the diet of the Mountain Gorilla.

Arundinaria anceps is cultivated in Europe for its attractive foliage.

Fig. 87 Mountain Bamboo (*Arundinaria alpina*)

HAGENIA or EAST AFRICAN ROSEWOOD
(*Hagenia abyssinica*)
Olboldo (Maa.)

Rose Family (*Rosaceae*)

Identification: A handsome tree to about 20 m tall, with reddish brown, flaky bark and large pinnate leaves in large terminal tufts. Individual leaflets are reddish when young, then pale green with silvery hairs on their undersurface, borne in 5 or 6 pairs plus a terminal leaflet, on long, hairy winged stalks. The heads of female flowers form in large reddish drooping masses, bulkier than the feathery, orange or white male flower heads.

Distribution: Indigenous to upland areas of eastern and southern Africa from Ethiopia and Uganda south to Malawi, Zambia and Zimbabwe, and west to the mountains of eastern Congo. Dominant, with *Hypericum* (p. 190) at the upper limits of bamboo and montane forest where *Hagenia-Hypericum* forms a distinct, park-like zone below the moorland. An indicator of the approach of the tree line, the trees can capture water from mist, allowing it to drip slowly to the floor.

Interest: Dried female flower heads and an infusion from the bark each yield a powerful medicine against intestinal worms. The wood is dark red, hard and used in carpentry.

Fig. 88 Hagenia (*Hagenia abyssinica*)

GIANT ST. JOHN'S-WORT (*Hypericum revolutum*)
Osasimwa (Maa.)

St. John's-wort Family (*Clusiaceae, or Guttiferae*)

Identification: A shrub or medium sized tree to 12 m, with hairless elliptical leaves about 25 mm long, and large, solitary bright yellow flowers which are borne at the end of branches. There are in our area at least 11 species of *Hypericum*, a huge genus that occurs almost worldwide comprising 425 species of annual and perennial herbs, shrubs and trees.

Distribution: Widespread in eastern and southern Africa, from Ethiopia, Uganda, Rwanda and the Congo southward to Tanzania, Mozambique, Zimbabwe and South Africa; also Madagascar and the Comoros. Found in riverine habitats, in dry evergreen forest and uplands; in montane environments, Giant St. John's-wort is a typical component, with *Hagenia* (p. 188), of the upper forest fringe and lower moorland among Tree Heath (p. 194) as a pioneer to forest.

Interest: A beautiful shrub for the garden that gives off a smell of curry (in South Africa, it is called the Curry Bush). Among the numerous species in cultivation, most come from Asia. One African species that merits more attention is *Hypericum bequaertii* that has spectacular orange, tulip-like flowers on frost-hardy trees at 4,000 m in the Rwenzori Mountains.

In medieval times, Monks dedicated the genus to St. John the Baptist but, in Europe *H. perforatum* in particular had been a pagan plant, hung about in houses in high summer as protection against evil spirits. Various species yield a good yellow dye, and a salve made to heal wounds, a virtue reflected in the French name 'Tout-Saine' meaning all-heal. *H. perforatum* possesses sedative and astringent properties and is widely used in homeopathy. Hyperforin-like constituents isolated from species including *H. revolutum* have been found cytotoxic to colon carcinoma, and anti-viral activity is shown by hypericin.

Fig. 89 Giant St. John's-Wort (*Hypericum revolutum*)

LION'S-CLAW, or CANARY BUSH
(*Crotalaria agatiflora*)
Olontwalan (Maa.)

Pea Family (*Fabaceae, Papilionaceae* or *Leguminosae* Sub-family *Papilionoideae*)

Identification: A bush, branched shrub or small tree to 10 m, with 3-foliolate leaves and large, strikingly attractive lemon-yellow flowers borne in clusters on stout stalks, looking like small yellow birds. In fact, the flowers are much visited by sunbirds. When dry, the pods rattle with their seed ('crotalan' means a rattle in Greek) before exploding with a loud 'crack'!

Distribution: Lion's-claw is widely distributed in East Africa, northwards to Ethiopia, eastwards to the Congo and southwards to Mozambique, found in margins and clearings of upland rainforest and riverine bushland. It is probably sunbird pollinated, and it is abundant and conspicuous when in flower around the rim of Ngorongoro Crater. There are some 550 species of *Crotalaria* throughout the tropics and sub-tropics nearly 400 of which are native to Africa.

Interest: Lion's-claw is grown for its decorative flowers. A root decoction is used locally for treating gonorrhoea. Many *Crotalaria* species are poisonous to livestock causing crotalism, possibly attributable to toxic alkaloids.

The Asian relative Sunn-hemp (*C. juncea*) is widely cultivated in East Africa (where it is known as marijea) both as a fibre crop and as a green manure: as a legume, it has the remarkable ability to capture atmospheric nitrogen and convert it into organic nitrogen compounds, through the combined actions of a symbiotic relationship with a bacterium (*Rhizobium*) present in nodules on the plant's root system.

Fig. 90 Lion's-Claw (*Crotalaria agatiflora*)

5. Moorland and Afro-alpine Flowers

TREE HEATH, or GIANT HEATH (*Erica arborea*)
Ol-kibejus (Maa.)

Heather Family (*Ericaceae*)

Identification: An evergreen, upright shrub or tree to 7 m, with bright green needle-like leaves in whorls of 3 or 4. The young twigs are hairy but the foliage is hairless. Bell-shaped, white flowers are scented and borne in large terminal heads.

The related *E. excelsa* (*Philippia*) differs in having 3-merous, not 4-merous, flowers.

Distribution: Co-dominant in moorland, above the *Hagenia-Hypericum* zone on East African mountains, but widely distributed and native in the Mediterranean eastwards to Asia Minor and the Caucasus.

An Ericaceous tree, with a gnarled trunk, broad leaves and greenish white flowers is *Agauria salicifolia*; there is a fine specimen at Saddle Hut on Mt. Meru as well as on the floor of Meru Crater.

Interest: Tree Heath is common in cultivation and has been used widely in the development of cultivars and hybrids. It is a parent of *E. x. veitchii*, for example. It is also an important plant for honey bees.

The word brier-wood (from the French "bruyere", for white heather) refers to the woody burls cut from the roots of Tree Heath for making tobacco pipes.

Fig. 91 Tree Heath (*Erica arborea*)

STOEBE (*Stoebe kilimandscharica*)
Ol-kibejus (Maa.)

Daisy Family (*Asteraceae, or Compositae*)

Identification: A heath-like shrub, 2-6 m tall, with very crowded, softly, hairy, needle leaves and rather drab, golden brown flowers borne in dense, tubular heads.

Distribution: From the bamboo and *Hagenia-Hypericum* zones of the upper forest to the moorland where Stoebe can become co-dominant with Tree Heath, on mountains including both Mt. Kenya and Kilimanjaro.

Interest: The related *Stoebe plumosa* is occasionally in cultivation in Europe.

Fig. 92 Stoebe (*Stoebe kilimandscharica*)

PROTEA, or SUGAR BUSH (*Protea caffra*)

Protea Family (*Proteaceae*)

Identification: Shrub or small tree to 3 m, with hard, leathery, evergreen and unstalked leaves with wavy, red margins. White or cream flowers are in large, terminal, solitary heads enclosed within green bracts that are often felty and rust-coloured outside.

Distribution: On rocky slopes in the *Hagenia* belt (p. 188) and in moorland, on Mt. Elgon, Mt. Kenya and Mt. Kilimanjaro (*P. kilimandscharica = P. caffra*). There are 3 species of *Protea* in Kenya and about 130 species in South Africa where they dominate the Cape flora. Their slow rate of growth and sparse seed production increase their tendency to become rare.

Important members of the Protea Family in East Africa include the Australian Silk-oak (*Grevillea robusta*) which is a very successful shade tree on coffee estates, and the Queensland-nut (*Macadamia ternifolia*) that is a highly prized confectionery nut.

Interest: Named after the Greek sea god, Proteus, whose wish to avoid recognition relied upon continuous changes in shape, the showy, colourfully bracted flower heads of Proteas exhibit an incredible degree of variation that makes them popular cut flowers. Heads contain copious nectar which attracts sunbirds and sugarbirds (*Promerops* spp.) by which Proteas are pollinated. In South Africa sugarbirds breed in *Protea* vegetation and use the fluff from inflorescences for their nests.

Fig. 93 Protea (*Protea caffra*)

BLUE DELPHINIUM, or LARKSPUR
(*Delphinium macrocentron*)

Buttercup Family (*Ranunculaceae*)

Identification: An upright, herbaceous perennial with deeply dissected leaves and a softy hairy stem up to 2 m tall. The showy flowers are borne in loose spikes, strikingly coloured turquoise blue and metallic green, each with a stout, ascending spur that contains nectar attractive to long-tongued insects.

Distribution: Found over a wide range of altitudes in upland Kenya and Tanzania, in moist rocky montane grassland and moorland, including Mt. Elgon, Mt. Kenya and Mt. Kilimanjaro. There are three other species of *Delphinium* in East Africa, including the white *D. leroyi* (p. 202).

Interest: Delphinium is a northern temperate genus of annuals (often referred now to *Consolida*) and perennials many of which are grown as decoratives for their spikes of showy, often blue, flowers. Most are of Asian and European origin. Striking scarlet flowered species include *D. nudicaule*, from California.

Delphinium species contain a poisonous alkaloid, delphinine, sometimes used as an insecticide reflected in the name 'Licebane' (*D. staphisagria*). In the western USA, stockmen have often referred to wild Delphinium as "Locoweed" because of a stagger that develops in sheep and cattle that feed on the plant.

Fig. 94 Blue Delphinium (*Delphinium macrocentron*)

WHITE DELPHINIUM or LARKSPUR
(*Delphinium leroyi*)

Buttercup Family (*Ranunculaceae*)

Identification: Like Blue Delphinium (p. 200), this is an upright perennial with dissected foliage, differing in its larger, sweetly fragant white flowers that have longer upcurving spurs.

Distribution: Widespread throughout eastern Africa, from southern Sudan, eastern Congo, Uganda and Kenya, southwards through Tanzania to Malawi, at altitudes up to about 2,200 m in montane grassland and burnt savannah woodland. Rather rare; found on the wall of Ngorongoro Crater, and on the Nyika Plateau where it appears occasionally to hybridize with the blue flowered *Delphinium dasycaulon*.

Interest: A very beautiful plant that would seem to have much potential as an ornamental. Probably poisonous.

Fig. 95 White Delphinium (*Delphinium leroyi*)

RED HOT POKER (*Kniphofia thomsonii*)

Lily Family (*Liliaceae*)

Identification: A handsome perennial with a fibrous rhizome from which arises a basal cluster of 100 cm-long, strap-shaped leaves and a tall inflorescence of elongated, trumpet-shaped flowers which vary in colour from yellow to flame red and are borne in a dense pendulous head.

Distribution: Widespread in eastern Africa from the Congo, Burundi, Uganda and Ethiopia to Kenya and Tanzania in a wide range of habitats including montane grassland, in marshes and along streams in upland.

A genus confined to Africa, southwards to the Cape with one species in Madagascar.

Interest: An important group of garden plants with numerous cultivars and hybrids some of which are derivatives of *Kniphofia thomsonii*. Visited by sunbirds which pollinate the Red Hot Poker.

Fig. 96 Red Hot Poker (*Kniphofia thomsonii*)

AFRICAN BLUE-EYED GRASS (*Aristea alata*)

Iris Family (*Iridaceae*)

Identification: An erect, tufted, rhizomatous perennial with fans of short, stiff basal leaves and an upright, branched inflorescence of clusters of bright blue flowers. The stem is flattened and narrowly winged.

Distribution: Locally common in wet, montane grassland from Ethiopia and the Congo southwards to Zimbabwe.

A fairly large genus that is confined to eastern and southern Africa, and Madagascar, allied to the northern temperate genus *Sisyrinchium*.

Interest: Related species including the South African *A. ecklonii* are grown for their attractive spikes of blue flowers.

Fig. 97 African Blue-eyed Grass (*Aristea alata*)

KENYAN SAND-CROCUS (*Romulea keniensis*)

Iris Family (*Iridaceae*)

Identification: Like a small Crocus with a stem arising out of the ground from a corm at flowering; it bears a solitary funnel-shaped flower that is mauve or pale purplish pink.

Distribution: In wet stony places along streams, and in short grassland in the alpine zones on Mt. Kenya, the Aberdares and Kilimanjaro; not known elsewhere. *Romulea fischeri*, with larger star-like flowers, is more common and more widely distributed in eastern Africa from Ethiopia and Uganda to Mt. Elgon and the Cherangani's in addition to Mt. Kenya and the Aberdares. Other species are found in southern Africa, and several are European.

Interest: Named after Romulus, the founder of Rome, because several *Romulea* species are Mediterranean. Various species, including yellow-flowered ones like *R. bulbocodium*, are cultivated for their flowers. Several are adapted to sandy habitats, giving the common name of Sand-crocus to the genus.

Fig. 98 Kenyan Sand-crocus (*Romulea keniensis*)

EVENING FLOWER (*Hesperantha petitiana*)

Iris Family (*Iridaceae*)

Identification: A small herb with narrow bristle-like leaves arising from a corm that is covered with scales. Flowers, which are either solitary or borne in a spike to about 30 cm high, are pink to pale mauve and funnel-shaped, with a yellow spot in the throat.

Distribution: Locally common in stony grassland in the alpine zone, on Mt. Elgon and Mt. Kenya, the Aberdares and Kilimanjaro, extending north to Sudan and Ethiopia, and south to the Nyika Plateau of Malawi and to Zimbabwe.

The genus *Hesperantha* is confined to tropical and southern Africa where other species including *H. bicolor* and *H. pulchra* occur.

Interest: Various species are grown for their attractive flowers, typically opening in the evening; they are sweetly scented at night. Their generic name comes from the Greek 'Hesperos' for evening.

Fig. 99 Evening Flower (*Hesperantha petitiana*)

AFRICAN HAREBELL, ANGEL'S FISHING ROD, or WANDFLOWER (*Dierama cupiflorum*)

Iris Family (*Iridaceae*)

Identification: A very handsome plant. An erect clump-forming corm with long, strap-shaped leaves and delicate, nodding, funnel-shaped flowers that are pale pinkish purple, borne on long, arching, wiry stems.

Distriction: Widespread and fairly common in montane grassland, from eastern Uganda and southern Ethiopia, through Kenya and Tanzania. Other species, including *D. pendulum* and the beautiful *D. pulcherrimum*, are among those found in southern Africa.

Interest: *Dierama* species are valuable decorative plants and a number of them are in cultivation.

Fig. 100 African Harebell (*Dierama cupiflorum*)

RED MOUNTAIN GLADIOLUS
(*Gladiolus watsonioides*)

Iris Family (*Iridaceae*)

Identification: A beautiful plant, the finest of the East African gladioli, with striking, bright red flowers with a long curved tube. Flowers are borne in a single spike on a leafy stem arising from a corm. Leaves are ribbed, flat and sword-shaped.

Distribution: Confined to high altitudes in wet, stony soils in the moorland and alpine zones of Mt. Kenya, the Aberdares, Kilimanjaro and Mt. Meru. Other species including *G. natalensis* (p. 118) occur at lower altitudes in East Africa, and other red-flowered gladioli like *G. cardinalis* are found at the Cape in South Africa where perhaps the greatest diversity of gladioli exists anywhere.

Interest: One of the most beautiful wild flowers in East Africa, rare in cultivation.

Fig. 101 Red Mountain Gladiolus (*Gladiolus watsonioides*)

LOBELIA (*Lobelia holstii*)

Bellflower Family (*Campanulaceae*)

Identification: A stiff perennial with ascending stems and lance-shaped, unstalked leaves. Flowers few, at the top of leafless stems, reddish, pinkish purple or mauve (but not blue, the common flower colour among lobelias).

Distribution: The commonest lobelia in our area, in rocky places in dry montane grassland in Kenya and Tanzania, with a range from Ethiopia to the Congo. Garden Lobelia (*L. erinus*), widely grown as an ornamental in window boxes and hanging baskets, is a native of South Africa. Giant species are described on pages 232.

Interest: Indian Tobacco (*Lobelia inflata*) is a blue flowered annual species native to North America. The dried leaves are the source of an alkaloid which has been used as an expectorant and emetic, and apparently also as an insecticide.

Fig. 102 Lobelia (*Lobelia holstii*)

SWERTIA (*Swertia crassiuscula*)

Gentian Family (*Gentianaceae*)

Identification: A creeping herbaceous perennial with narrow-based leaves with broad, rounded tips, borne in a dense, tightly compact rosette from which arise conspicuous white, to very pale pink, flowers on short stalks.

Distribution: In montane flushes, and in wet, shallow and stony soils in moorland and the lower alpine zone on Kilimanjaro, Meru, Mt. Kenya, Elgon and the Aberdares, sometimes locally abundant. Among the 14 other species of *Swertia* in East Africa, *S. kilimandscharica* is also widespread; it has large white to pale blue flowers on erect stems.

Interest: Marsh Felwort (*S. perennis*), a European montane species, is occasionally cultivated. Chirata (*S. chirata*) has been used in herbal medicine as an appetite and liver stimulant, and as an antimalarial.

Fig. 103 Swertia (*Swertia crassiuscula*)

MOUNTAIN PIMPERNEL (*Anagallis serpens*)

Primrose Family (*Primulaceae*)

Identification: A small, trailing plant with oval leaves and conspicuous, pink flowers on short stalks. One of 12 species of *Anagallis* in East Africa where the Scarlet Pimpernel (*A. arvensis*) is an introduced weed.

Distribution: Common in alpine and sub-alpine streamside marshes, in the Aberdares, on Mt. Elgon, Mt. Kenya and Kilimanjaro. Also in Ethiopia.

Interest: None known for *A. serpens*. Its relative, *A. arvensis*, is long known as a combined sundial and weather glass (e.g. "Shepherd's Weather-glass", "Old Man's Weather-vane"), opening its petals at 8.00 am and closing them at about 2.00 pm, or if weather becomes dull. Extracts of pimpernel have been used medicinally to stimulate the flow of bile, and in the treatment of snake bite, epilepsy, hypochondria and manic depression. Constituents include cucurbitacins, glycosides and saponins, and action includes diuretic, hepatic and antitussive (against coughs).

Fig. 104 Mountain Pimpernel (*Anagallis serpens*)

RWENZORI STONECROP (*Sedum ruwenzoriense*)

Stonecrop Family (*Crassulaceae*)

Identification: A trailing or erect perennial with softly woody stems and blunt, cylindrical fleshy leaves. Flowers are bright yellow, borne in diffuse, terminal heads.

Distribution: Common in rock crevices in moorland and lower alpine zones in the High Cheranganis, the Aberdares and Mt. Kenya. Also in Uganda, the Sudan, Congo and Rwanda. *S. meyeri-johannis*, a similar yellow-flowered stonecrop, differs in being herbaceous not woody at the base; it is an epiphyte in highland mist-forest, as on Kilimanjaro and Mt. Meru. Both resemble *S. acre* that is a widespread European species.

Interest: None, though the large genus *Sedum* comprises many species of decorative importance as alpines. *S. acre* is Biting Stonecrop or Wall-pepper known in Britain also as "Welcome-home-husband-though-never-so-drunk", probably due to its presence sometimes on roofs! It has a strong, acrid, peppery taste and has been added to salads.

Fig. 105 Rwenzori Stonecrop (*Sedum ruwenzoriense*)

HEBENSTRETIA (*Hebenstretia angolensis =
H. dentata*)

Figwort Family (*Scrophulariaceae*)

Identification: An erect, hairless, wiry sub-shrub
with alternate, linear leaves and long, terminal
spikes of creamy white tubular flowers, each with
an orange splash.

Distribution: Common in rocky moorland, and
occasional in dry grassland at lower altitudes in
East Africa. In Kenya, in the Cheranganis, the
Aberdares, on Mt. Kenya and Mt. Elgon; on Kilimanjaro
and Meru in Tanzania. A widespread plant, from
Ethiopia and the Congo southward to Malawi,
Mozambique, Zambia and Zimbabwe.

Interest: None.

Fig. 106 Hebenstretia (*Hebenstretia angolensis*)

HAPLOCARPHA (*Haplocarpha rueppellii*)

Daisy Family (*Asteraceae,* or *Compositae*)

Identification: A stemless herbaceous perennial with a rosette of large, shiny leaves that are pressed close to the ground, white-woolly below dark green above. Their outline is variable: oval, triangular or round, either toothed or un-toothed (but not lobed, as in *H. schimperi*). The rich yellow flowers are borne in unstalked solitary heads.

Distribution: An alpine of frost-prone areas up to 4,000 m, often on loose soils, on Mts. Kilimanjaro, Kenya and Elgon. Also in Ethiopia.

Interest: Haplocarpha has adapted to unstable soil conditions that prevail in high altitudes in the alpine zone by developing a stout tap root which makes the plant less susceptible to disturbance caused by frost heaving of the soil surface. Seedling establishment must be precarious. Haplocarpha has overcome this problem through geocarpy: burial of the fruit while still attached to the mother plant.

Fig. 107 Haplocarpha (*Haplocarpha rueppellii*)

EURYOPS (*Euryops dacrydiodes*)

Daisy Family (*Asteraceae*, or *Compositae*)

Identification: A bushy shrub to about 1 m, with dark green scale-like leaves that are pressed closely to the up-right branches and with solitary heads of bright yellow flowers.

Distribution: Common in the moorland and alpine zones on Kilimanjaro. *E. brownei*, with crowded linear leaves, is the common species in Kenya (Mt. Kenya, Aberdares) whereas *E. elgonensis*, which has broader leaves, is confined to Mt. Elgon. *E. jacksonii* occurs in rocky places in dry uplands (e.g. Rift Valley); *E. galpinii* is found at the Cape.

Interest: A large African genus of shrubs some of which are cultivated for their showy yellow flowers; ornamentals include *E. acraeus* and *E. pectinatus*.

Fig. 108 Euryops (*Euryops dacrydiodes*)

MOUNTAIN THISTLE (*Carduus keniensis*)

Daisy Family (*Asteraceae*, or *Compositae*)

Identification: A conspicuous, spiny rosette plant with large, divided oblong leaves. The pinkish flowers are borne on a single central stem, with the heads embedded in a dense straw-coloured spiny mass.

Distribution: Widespread in moorland on Mt. Kilimanjaro, Meru, the Aberdares, Mt. Elgon and Mt. Kenya where it occurs in tussocky grassland. There are 8 other species of *Carduus* in East Africa, all above 1,500 m altitude.

Interest: None.

Fig. 109 Mountain Thistle (*Carduus keniensis*)

GIANT GROUNDSEL (*Senecio johnstonii* ssp. *cottonii*)

Daisy Family (*Asteraceae,* or *Compositae*)

Identification: The Giant Groundsels are among the most spectacular mountain plants that belong to the immense genus *Senecio* that occurs world-wide. Giant Groundsels are shrubs or trees to 9 m, often with branched stems that end in a dense rosette of large robust leaves. As branches grow, the lower ring of leaves turns yellow and dies but remains attached, forming a thick lagging around the trunk. The bark is deeply furrowed and corky. Flowering is rare and may occur at 10-20 year intervals, when magnificent panicles of bright yellow flowers appear.

Distribution: Giant Groundsels derive from lower altitudes on African mountains where they are the most similar; the most distinct occur in the alpine zones on separate mountain tops, having evolved and adapted to ever harsher climates. *S. johnstonii* is a variable species with many geographical subspecies: *S. johnstonii* ssp. *cottonii* is confined to Kilimanjaro; ssp. battiscombei is found only on Mt. Kenya, the Aberdares and the Cherangani Hills; ssp. *elgonensis* is endemic to Mt. Elgon. The closely related *S. keniodendron* is common in the alpine belt of Mt. Kenya and the Aberdares. In general, forms on the drier, cooler mountains to the East (Kilimanjaro, Mt. Kenya) tend to have enlarged rosettes on fewer, thicker stems than forms on the wetter, more westerly mountains (Elgon, Rwenzori) of East Africa.

Interest: Alpine plants of temperate latitudes are often compact cushions whereas Afro-alpines like Giant Groundsel have evolved as giants, with mechanisms (like lagging of trunks with dead leaves, and the protection of buds with a thick slime that acts as anti-freeze) to counteract not the seasonal but the *diurnal* fluctuations in temperature.

Many species of *Senecio* are well-known for their poisonous properties. Ragwort (*S. jacobaea*), which contains the alkaloid jacobine, causes insidious and irreversible cirrhosis of the liver and is the great enemy of horse keepers.

Fig. 110 Giant Groundsel (*Senecio johnstonii* ssp. *cottonii*)

CABBAGE GROUNDSEL (*Senecio keniensis* ssp. *keniensis,* = *S. brassica*)

Daisy Family (*Asteraceae,* or *Compositae*)

Identification: A dwarf form of the giant groundsel sub-genus (*Dendrosenecio*), thin stemmed, creeping and rooting, but up to 1.8 m when in bloom. Flower-heads are bright yellow, and both ray and tube florets are present. The larger, densely felty leaves are carried at ground level so that its rosettes look like giant cabbages.

Distribution: Moist, swampy sites confined to Mt. Kenya.

Interest: Cabbage Groundsel guards its central buds from frost by folding its leaves over each night. The outer leaves become frozen, but they can withstand that, and the tender terminal bud (which cannot) is safe within.

Fig. 111 Cabbage Groundsel (*Senecio keniensis*)

ROSE GROUNDSEL (*Senecio roseiflorus*)

Daisy Family (*Asteraceae,* or *Compositae*)

Identification: An erect densely glandular herb or weak shrub with unstalked, oblong, lobed leaves and terminal, flat-topped heads of purple rayed florets.

Distribution: Locally common in drier moorland in the Aberdares and on Mt. Kenya; unknown elsewhere.

Interest: None.

Fig. 112 Rose Groundsel (*Senecio roseiflorus*)

BLUE BOG LOBELIA (*Lobelia deckenii*)

Bellflower Family (*Campanulaseae*)

Identification: A stemless rosette plant with oval to lance-shaped leaves in tightly packed spirals, and a hollow, erect spike of purple flowers.

Distribution: Like the Giant Groundsels (p. 232), the Blue Bog Lobelia has also speciated and there are six different sub-species on six different mountain massifs, a radiation that may have occurred in less than one million years. Sub-species keniensis, to 3 m tall, is confined to Mt. Kenya above 3,000 m where it is common in marshes; ssp. *sattimae* is confined to swamps in the Aberdares; and ssp. deckenii, which is much taller, is endemic to Kilimanjaro. The related *L. bequaertii* is a giant bog species found on Rwenzori. In contrast, *L. gibberoa* is a widespread, woody species of forest margins at lower altitudes in many montane areas.

Interest: The leaf rosettes hold pools of water in which live fly larvae that are important in the diet of the Scarlet-tufted Malachite Sunbird which visits the flowers and pollinates them. Each night, a plate of ice forms over the pool of liquid acting as a shield to the water beneath which doesn't freeze and the submerged bud survives undamaged. By day, the water in the pool is protected from the hot sun by the plant's secretion of a slime that hinders evaporation.

Fig. 113 Blue Bog Lobelia (*Lobelia deckenii*)

MOUNT KENYA GIANT LOBELIA (*Lobelia telekii*)

Bellflower Family (*Campanulaceae*)

Identification: Similar to the Blue Bog Lobelia but which grows to 4 m tall. Leaves are very long and narrow and flower stems have long, feathery bracts which hang down and hide the small pale blue flowers within them. It is a spectacular plant looking like a furry pillar. Patrick Synge described them beautifully as "great petrified woolly bears"!

Distribution: In wet, stony ground at 3,000 m on Mt. Elgon, Mt. Kenya and the Aberdares, at altitudes at which the feathery bracts form a thick air-trapping muff that protects against the frost at night. *L. telekii* is also adapted to the comparatively dry conditions that prevail on these easterly massifs, relative to the much wetter conditions that occur further west in the Rwenzori Mountains, where the similar *L. wollastonii* is found.

Interest: Together with the Giant Groundsels, the Giant Lobelias are among the most spectacular mountain plants, their great size is in remarkable contrast to the lobelias of lower altitude (like *L. holstii*, p. 216) and of other parts of the world. In the Andes, members of both the daisy family (*Espeletia* spp., 'Frailejon') and the pineapple family (*Puya* spp.) have developed into giants in a similar way.

Fig. 114 Mount Kenya Giant Lobelia (*Lobelia telekii*)

ALPINE ROCK-CRESS (*Arabis alpina*)

Cabbage Family (*Brassicaceae,* or *Cruciferae*)

Identification: A perennial, mat-forming herb with hairy, oblong, toothed leaves and small white flowers each with four narrow petals.

Distribution: Common above 3,000 m in East Africa, often along streambanks and on cliffs. This arctic montane species is widely distributed, from boreal America to much of Europe and Siberia, in arctic wastes and on moist montane rocks and gravels, showing remarkably little variation over its vast, discontinuous range.

Interest: Closely related to Garden Arabis (*A. caucasica*; sometimes considered a sub-species of *A. alpina*), with larger fragrant white (or pink) flowers.

Fig. 115 Alpine Rock-cress (*Arabis alpina*)

EVERLASTING FLOWER (*Helichrysum newii*)

Daisy Family (*Asteraceae,* or *Compositae*)

Identification: A small bushy shrub, greyish silver with matted hairs, bearing narrow elliptic, un-stalked, crowded leaves and large solitary terminal white heads. The flower-heads comprise enlarged, persistent shiny bracts within which the flowers themselves are rather inconspicuous.

Distribution: Common at high altitudes on Kilimanjaro and Meru, often forming a characteristic scrub. Also in alpine stony heathland on Mt. Elgon, Mt. Kenya and in the Aberdares. About 80 species of *Helichrysum* in East Africa among a large, widespread genus found also in South Africa, Australasia, Asia and Europe.

Interest: Among the many species in cultivation, *H. bracteatum* has papery, double flower-heads of various colours and is the species widely used as the Everlasting Flower of florists. *H. petiolare* is grown in hanging baskets and as ground cover for its trailing, silvery shoots and grey-felted leaves. *H. serotinum* is the Curry Plant.

Fig. 116 Everlasting Flower (*Helichrysum newii*)

GLOSSARY

Biodiversity. Biological diversity; the array of all living things and the interactions between them.

Ecosystem. A unit of vegetation, its associated animals, and the physico-chemical components of their immediate environment that together form a recognisable, self-contained entity, or system.

Edaphic. Relating to the physical, chemical and biological characteristics of the soil.

Endemic. Confined to one particular area.

Epiphyte. A plant attached to another plant, not growing parasitically on it but using it merely for support.

Genus (plural Genera). A group of related species sharing similar characteristics.

Geocarpy. Burial of fruit while still attached to the plant.

Habitat. Place with a particular kind of environment inhabited by particular plants and animals. The whole complex of environmental factors which differentiate units of vegetation.

Herb. A non-woody herbaceous plant (as opposed to a woody shrub or tree).

Kopje. Inselberg; a tumbled mass of boulders, usually intrusions of granite.

Mopane. Woodland dominated by the legume tree *Colophospermum mopane* that occurs at lower altitudes in southern tropical Africa, from northern Zambia southwards.

Obovate. As in a leaf, broadest above the middle.

Ovate. As in a leaf, broadest below the middle.

Paramo. Moorland at high altitude in the Andes, where 'frailejones' (*Espeletia* spp.) have remarkable resemblance to the Giant Groundsels (*Senecio* spp.) characteristic of East African mountains.

Solifluction. Movements of soil material brought about by continual freezing and thawing.

Speciation. Process by which a new species arises.

Species. The basic unit of plant and animal classification. A group of like individuals able to interbreed and produce fertile offspring.

Succession. The orderly sequence in which plants colonise a piece of ground, one kind replacing another, until those best suited to the prevailing circumstances survive and all the rest die out.

Symbiosis. A living together of dissimilar organisms to their mutual advantage.

Trifoliolate. Of a leaf, made up of three leaflets.

Umbel. An inflorescence (flower head) in which all individual flower stalks arise from a single point.

Xerophytic. Adapted to dry areas, with ability to recover from partial dessication or to internal storage of water.

REFERENCES AND FURTHER READING

Agnew, A.D.Q. (1974). *Upland Kenya Wild Flowers.* Oxford University Press, London UK, 827pp.

Agnew, A.D.Q. and Hedberg. O. (1969). Geocarpy as an adaptation to Afroalpine solifluction soils. *Journal of the East African Natural History Society and National Museum* 27, 215-216.

Attenborough, D. (1985). *The Living Planet.* Fontana/Collins/BBC, London, UK, 320pp.

Attenborough, D. (1995). *The Private Life of Plants.* BBC, London, UK, 320pp.

Baker, S.J.K. (1963). The East African environment, in Oliver, R. and Mathew, G. (eds.). *History of East Africa*, pp. 1-22. Clarendon, Oxford, UK.

Beentje, H. (1994). *Kenya Trees, Shrubs and Lianas.* National Museums of Kenya, Nairobi, Kenya, 722pp.

Bigger, M. (1966). A guide to the wild flowers of Kilimanjaro. *Ice Cap 4*, Journal of The Kilimanjaro Mountain Club.

Blundell, M. (1982). *The Wild Flowers of Kenya.* Collins, London, UK, 160pp.

Blundell, M. (1987). *Collins Guide to the Wild Flowers of East Africa.* Collins, London UK, 464pp.

Chapman, J. (2002). Barking up the right tree. *Plant Life*, Spring 2002, p.15.

Coates Palgrave, K. (1977). *Trees of Southern Africa.* Struik, Cape Town, South Africa, 959pp.

Coe, M.J. (1967). *The Ecology of the Alpine Zone of Mount Kenya.* W. Junk, The Hague, The Netherlands, 136pp.

Coe, M., McWilliam, N., Stone, G. and Packer, M. (eds.) (1999). *Mkomazi: The Ecology, Biodiversity and Conservation of a Tanzanian Savanna.* Royal Geographical Society, London, UK, 620pp.

Drummond, R.B. and Coates Palgrave, K. (1973). *Common Trees of the Highveld.* Longman, Harare, Zimbabwe, 99pp.

Drummond, R.B. (1984). *Arable Weeds of Zimbabwe.* Agricultural Research Trust, Harare, Zimbabwe, 154pp.

Eggeling, W.J. (1940). *The Indigenous Trees of the Uganda Protectorate.* Government Press, Entebbe, Uganda, 296pp.

Everard, B and Morley, B.D. (1970). *Wild Flowers of the World.* Ebury Press and Michael Joseph, London, UK, 432pp.

Greenway, P.J. and Vesey-Fitzerald, D.F. (1969). The vegetation of Lake Manyara National Park. Journal of Ecology 57, 127-149.

Gwynne, M.D. and Bell, R.H.V. (1968). Selection of vegetation components by grazing ungulates in the Serengeti National Park. *Nature 220*, 390-393.

Hanby, J. and Bygott, D. (n.d.) *Ngorongoro Conservation Area.* David Bygott & Co., Karatu, Tanzania, 84pp.

Hanby, J., Snelson, D. and Bygott, D. (1987). *Kilimanjaro National Park.* Tanzania National Parks, Arusha, Tanzania/African Wildlife Foundation, Nairobi, Kenya, 60pp.

Herlocker, D (1968). *Ngorongoro's Trees and Shrubs.* Ngorongoro Conservation Unit, Tanzania, 26pp.

Heriz-Smith, S. (1962). *The Wild Flowers of the Nairobi Royal National Park*. D. A. Hawkins Ltd., Nairobi, Kenya.

Jex-Blake, M. (1948). *Some Wild Flowers of Kenya*, Highway Press, Nairobi, Kenya, 155pp.

Kingdon, J. (1990). *Island Africa: The Evolution of Africa's Rare Animals and Plants*. Collins, London, UK, 287pp.

Lyogello, L.N. (1988). *A Guide to Tanzania National Parks*. Tanzania Tourist Guide Books, Dar es Salaam, Tanzania, 263pp.

Matthiessen, P. (1984). *The Tree Where Man was Born*. Picador, London, UK, 256pp.

Moriarty, A. (1975). Wild Flowers of Malawi. Purnell, Cape Town, South Africa, 166pp.

Newall, C.A., Anderson, L.A. and Phillipson, J.D. (1996). *Herbal Medicines: a guide for health-care professionals*. The Pharmaceutical Press, London, UK. 296pp.

Newton, P. and Wolfe, N. (1992). Can animals teach us medicine? *British Medical Journal* 305: 1517-1518.

Noad, T. and Birnie, A. (1989). *Trees of Kenya*. Noad and Birnie, Nairobi, Kenya, 308pp.

Piers, F. (1968). *Orchids of East Africa*. J. Cramer, Lehre, Germany, 304pp.

Redhead, J. (1981). The Mazumbai Forest: an island of lower montane rain forest in the West Usambaras. *African Journal of Ecology 19*, 195-199.

Rodgers, W.A and Homewood, K.M. (1982). Species richness and endemism in the Usambara mountain forests, Tanzania. *Biological Journal of the Linnean Society 18*, 197-242.

Roodt, V. (2005). *The Tourist Travel and Field Guide of the Ngorongoro Conservation Area*. Papyrus Publications, Pretoria, South Africa, 184pp.

Sapieha, T. (n.d.) *Wayside Flowers of Kenya*. Wayside Flowers of Kenya, Nairobi, 108pp.

Scott, J. (1988). *The Great Migration*. Elm Tree, London, UK. 159pp.

Snelson, D. and Bygott, D. (1986)a. *Lake Manyara National Park*. Tanzania National Parks, Arusha, Tanzania/African Wildlife Foundation, Nairobi, Kenya. 44pp.

Snelson, D. and Bygott, D. (1986)b. *Serengeti National Park*. Tanzania National Parks, Arusha, Tanzania/African Wildlife Foundation, Nairobi, Kenya, 72pp.

Snelson, D. and Bygott, D. (1987). *Arusha National Park*. Tanzania National Parks, Arusha, Tanzania/African Wildlife Foundation, Nairobi, Kenya, 52pp.

Snelson, D. and Scott, J. (1986). *Tarangire National Park*. Tanzania National Parks, Arusha, Tanzania/African Wildlife Foundation, Nairobi, Kenya, 56pp.

Verdcourt, B and Trump, E.C. (1969). *Common Poisonous Plants of East Africa*. Collins, London, UK, 254pp.

Vesey-Fitzgerald, D (1973). *East African Grasslands*. East African Publishing House, Nairobi, Kenya, 95pp.

Williams, J.G. (1967). *A Field Guide to the National Parks of East Africa*. Collins, London, UK, 352pp.